Psychological Astrology and the Twelve Houses

By Noel Eastwood

Psychotherapist, Astrologer, Tarotist

Also by Noel Eastwood:

Astrology of Health: physical and psychological health in the natal and progressed chart

The Fool's Journey through the Tarot Major Arcana

The Fool's Journey through the Tarot Pentacles

The Fool's Journey through the Tarot Swords

The Fool's Journey through the Tarot Cups

The Fool's Journey through the Tarot Wands

Self Hypnosis Tame Your Inner Dragons: clinical and psychic use of trance

Psychological Astrology and the Signs of the Zodiac – due late 2018

Psychological Astrology and the Planets of Power – due 2019

Why not subscribe to my weekly newsletter?

Visit www.plutoscave.com

Facebook: www.facebook.com/plutoscave

IMPORTANT LEGAL NOTICE

This book is intended to give the student of astrology insight into the psychological imprint of the twelve astrological Houses. It also seeks to demonstrate how to deepen your understanding of your natal chart through meditation using the symbols of astrology. It is stressed that the contents of this book are in no way a substitute for personal supervision by a qualified medical or psychological professional. It is recommended that you consult your health professional if you wish to compliment your treatment with meditation, astrology or the techniques described here. This book is not a substitute for psychotherapy or counseling, if you have an underlying psychological condition or are in crisis, please seek professional help. As we cannot assess your mental state, the author, editors and publishers accept no responsibility for outcomes if you use the techniques described in this book.

To protect the privacy of certain individuals their names and identifying details have been changed.

This book is copyrighted. Apart from any fair use for the purposes of private study, research, criticism or review as permitted by the Copyright Act, no part may be reproduced without written permission of the author.

Inquiries should be addressed to Noel Eastwood:

Web site: www.plutoscave.com

Email: info@plutoscave.com

Copyright © Noel Eastwood 2015

Editor: Maria Pocsai-Faglin

Front cover: The Archetype of Libra by Peta Fenton

Contents

To Steph, of Astrologer's Forum and my good friend and Druid, Peter Cato, thank you both for your friendship and generous support. I would also like to give a special 'thank you' to Chris Turner, my wonderful astrology teacher; and to my editor, Maria, for her tireless work in getting this book from concept to publication.

Introduction

The astrological birth chart is known as a **Horoscope** or a **Natal chart** or just **chart**. We refer to the person whose horoscope we are reading as the **native**. Each chart requires three things: your **date**, **place** and **time** of **birth**. An accurate birth time, to within 10 minutes, shows which zodiac Sign is above you at the time of your birth (Midheaven), and which is on your eastern horizon (Ascendant). In this book you will learn why it is so important to know these two Signs.

You will learn the Significance of all 12 Houses and the relevance of their Cusps, those special lines that divide the chart into 12 sections, just like a pizza. Each House represents specific psychological factors, traits and characteristics. It can also indicate the people you attract and are attracted to. The Houses are used for forecasting purposes as well, but that's for another book.

This volume is the first in a series of three books introducing psychological astrology. In this part, the focus is specifically on the Houses of the horoscope; we will explore how and why they are created and how they help you understand yourself and others.

I will explore how each House can be understood personally and psychologically. My own personal meditations are here to demonstrate exactly how I use the astrological chart for my own spiritual development: I start by imagining myself going into the House and connecting with the archetypes on the cusp and within the House itself.

When I have an accurate birth time, date and place, I can begin to uncover the psychological urges and instincts of that person. This is extremely useful in my psychotherapy practice.

It is a good idea to have your own chart at hand and use it to help you better understand this book. If you don't have one, go to my web site and create it for free – www.plutoscave.com

Introduction to the Twelve Houses

The Houses correspond to the twelve Signs of the zodiac. For instance, the 1st House naturally corresponds to Aries, the first Sign; the 2nd House corresponds to Taurus, the 2nd Sign, etc. Keywords are generally interchangeable between the two, Houses and Signs, but there are subtle differences.

The Houses are like setting the stage for a play, it is this scene that forms the background to the story being told by the players (the Planets). Psychologically, they represent fields of human endeavour, they provide a context allowing the Planets to express their unique qualities.

Each **House Element**, corresponds to its own zodiac Sign. For instance, the Signs are divided into groups: Cardinal, Fixed and Mutable. The Houses are Angular, Succedent and Cadent.

Cardinal / Angular traits are being active, forward moving, adventurous and goal oriented (signs Aries, Cancer, Libra, Capricorn - Houses 1st, 4th, 7th, 10th)

Fixed / Succedent qualities are being solid, determined, dedicated and focused on achieving goals (signs Taurus, Leo, Scorpio, Aquarius - Houses 2nd, 5th, 8th, 11th)

Mutable / Cadent traits are working towards completion, finishing, rounding off and extending beyond what was begun at the Angular/Cardinal stage (signs Gemini, Virgo, Sagittarius, Pisces - Houses 3rd, 6th, 9th, 12th)

If we consider life as an unfolding narrative, a House represents where each story or chapter is experienced. As life events unfold they happen within a House: it is the backdrop, the atmosphere, the artifacts and the props, all in one. Houses provide the setting where the Planets perform their role. As William Shakespeare wrote, *"All the world's a stage, and all the men and women merely players: they have their exits and their entrances; and one man in his time plays many parts..."* [1]

The Houses are the stage of life, the Planets are the actors with their many exits and entrances, they work to define and build your life. The Houses are the WHERE, and the Planets are the WHAT.

When a Planet resides or sits in a House it shows where its activities are focused. For instance, let's consider the Moon in the 5th House. The Moon represents mothering and nurturing qualities, social engagement and natural innate emotional traits and needs. The 5th House is where these qualities will be expressed more immediately than anywhere else in the chart.

We therefore expect to see nurturing qualities expressed within the person's social circle, with their children and, in some cases, pets. They will nourish their friends, fuss over kids like a mother, and prefer to mingle within their own group, forming strong emotional attachments there. Also, they will tend to express their creativity in an area that involves nurturing and friendship.

The Planet is the actor and the House is the stage where they perform. If we take this one step further, the more Planets in a particular House, the greater their impact on WHERE the native will act out a particular planetary theme, trait and quality. The more Planets in a House, the more central the affairs and circumstances of that House.

This is why astrologers pay special attention to Planet groupings within Houses and Signs. A group of four or more Planets in a House forms a **stellium**. A stellium shows that this particular House provokes central themes and settings the native will return to again and again.

For instance, a stellium of Planets in the 5th House indicates that the person will focus on their friendships, creativity and fun or sporty activities. They will continually return to the themes of this House to define and re-define their identity. This implies a unique, creative expression of their needs in their own 5th House themes or that of their children (such as writing, art, sports, Facebook, fun, parties, etc.).

In these situations, planetary stelliums in Signs or Houses represent powerful unconscious urges and instincts propelling the native to seek an understanding and balance of these driving forces within that particular environment.

When a native has their Planets scattered in many different Houses, it shows that they seek a broad experience of life in various settings. We might say that they are generalists, while those with stelliums are specialists. A House without Planets does not mean that the native is not active in that domain, instead, it suggests that they have many things on their mind and that House environment in itself will not receive special attention. They may have a more relaxed approach towards the affairs of that particular House. More about this when we explore the Planets.

Point to remember: a stellium in a House provides insight into WHERE the native acts out the psychological needs, urges and instinctive drives of that particular Planet.

Direction of movement - the natal chart wheel and the Planet directions

All of the Planets in your chart travel in an anti-clockwise direction. The North Node (a.k.a. **NN**), however, travels clockwise, which is the same direction as the outer wheel of the natal chart.

To remind you, the Planets that astrologers use are:

The Sun and **Moon** - we also call them Luminaries

Mercury, Venus and **Mars** - called the Personal or Inner Planets

Jupiter, Saturn - the Outer Planets, Jupiter is also called the Bridging Planet because he bridges the Inner Planets with the Outer Planets

Chiron - an asteroid or dwarf Planet – he is so powerful that I always include him in my work

Uranus, Neptune and **Pluto** - these are called Outer or Generational Planets

The Planets orbit the Sun at various speeds, some take one year, others take hundreds of years. The Moon, of course, orbits the Earth and completes one rotation in roughly 28 days. Although many of these Planets are NOT Planets as such, nevertheless the correct astrological term is "Planets", for convenience.

We also use the Moon's Node, an angle of the Moon as it orbits the Earth. It is called the **North Node** and represents destiny or fate. We can use its opposite node, the **South Node**, but more about that later.

Each Planet appears in the sky against the backdrop of the fixed stars. These stars don't visibly move, but they do form interesting patterns called 'constellations', and twelve of them make our 'Signs of the zodiac'.

Thus each Planet travels around the Solar System at their own speed and viewed from the Earth, they appear to be moving past each constellation. We place these Planets in the natal chart in a circle representing their orbit around the Sun. Every day the Planets are in slightly different positions, occasionally they appear to stand still or go backwards. Sometimes they move but a tiny fraction of one degree.

Behind the Planets are the Signs of the zodiac: Leo, Virgo, Aquarius etc. We would say that a Planet, for instance Mars, is in Virgo in the 7th House. This means that Mars, in its orbit around the Sun, can be seen from Earth as it passes the constellation of Virgo, which appears behind it.

In **Barack Obama's** chart, Mars sits in his 7th House: it was just above the western horizon at the time of his birth.

How do we know that Mars was above the western horizon at the time of Obamas's birth? Simple, the Ascendant <=> Descendant line symbolizes the skyline.

Point to remember: in the natal chart the Planets move in an anti-clockwise direction, the chart wheel and the NN in a clockwise direction.

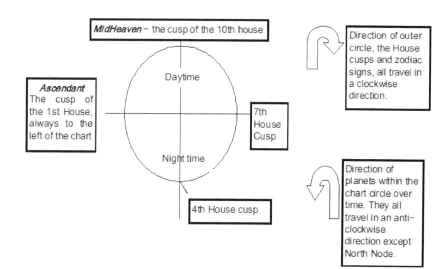

MidHeaven – the cusp of the 10th house

Daytime

Ascendant
The cusp of the 1st House, always to the left of the chart

7th House Cusp

Night time

4th House cusp

Direction of outer circle, the House cusps and zodiac signs, all travel in a clockwise direction.

Direction of planets within the chart circle over time. They all travel in an anti-clockwise direction except North Node.

The Astrological House Systems - Tropical and Sidereal

The Sun and the orbiting Planets move against the backdrop of the stars we call the Signs of the Zodiac. The Spring Equinox moves about 1° (1 degree) every 72 years. This is the very first degree of Aries and the beginning of Spring in the Northern Hemisphere.

The 1° shift was discovered by the Greek astronomer, Hipparchus (190 - 120 BC). He found that the Equinox moved 1° retrograde, or backwards. In other words, 0°Aries once coincided with the actual position of the constellation of Aries on the very first day of Spring. Now this occurs in the Sign of Pisces.

Hipparchus realised that the horoscope needed to be anchored somewhere, so he invented the Tropical Zodiac. This means that 0° Aries is permanently anchored in the zodiac at a single point, the day of the Spring Equinox.

Western astrologers use Hipparchus' Tropical Zodiac system, it is the most common astrological system practiced in Europe, America, Australia, etc. The Tropical System has allocated each Zodiac Sign exactly 30°. That means that Aries is exactly 30°, Leo is exactly 30°, Capricorn is exactly 30°... in fact all twelve zodiac Signs are exactly 30°. It is essential to understand this fact if you want to become an astrologer.

ALL Signs of the Zodiac are fixed at exactly 30°. The Houses, however, are not limited to any size.

Sidereal astrology is practiced by Indian and Arabic astrologers and is often called Vedic or Hindu Astrology. They use the REAL or actual position of the constellations. Each Sign / Constellation varies in size. For instance Aries begins on the 21st March and ends on the 20th April in the Tropical system. In the Hindu system it begins on the

15th April and ends on the 15th May. The current difference between the two systems is about 24°.

Point to Remember: Western or Tropical astrologers have fixed the size of their Signs to exactly 30°. The Sidereal or Hindu astrologers use varied Sign sizes according to where they are at the moment. The two systems give basically the same reading but come from a slightly different perspective.

Tropical astrology, which we will use in this book, fixes all the zodiac Signs to the same size, 30° each. They are fixed in the chart and are not attached to the actual position of the stars. Tropical astrologers do recognise the Precession of the Equinoxes (72 years for 1°) and this is why we say that we are heading towards the Aquarian age.

The Planets touch each zodiac Sign as they travel around our Solar System orbiting our Sun. Each Planet will therefore be in a different Constellation or Zodiac Sign at different times during their trajectory.

There are 88 named constellations today, Tropical astrologers use only 12 of them.

The Stars stay fixed, they hardly change their position (1° every 72 years), it is the Planets that move. These stars form patterns called the Constellations or Signs of the Zodiac. Each Sign represents a Greek mythological story. For instance the constellation of Leo (Latin for Lion) comes from the story of the Greek hero, Hercules, who slew the Nemean Lion during his Twelve Labours.

We use the Roman names for our astrological Signs and Planets. The Romans borrowed their myths from the Greeks. Thus Heracles (Greek) is the Roman Hercules. Evidence shows that the ancient Mesopotamians recorded the constellation of Leo as early as 4000

BC (that's 6000 years ago).

From now on all astrological discussion relates to the Tropical system of Western Astrology.

The Precession of the Equinoxes - The Age of Aquarius

Hipparchus observed that the Sun had a cycle of 25,868 years to complete one orbit of the entire zodiac, a complete circle. The Earth itself has a slight wobble and this contributes to the Aries point or Equinox changing slightly, about 1° every 72 years. When the Sun reaches the Equator, this is the Equinox, the warming of one hemisphere and the cooling of the other.

The Spring Equinox marks an important event, it is the rebirth of the Sun after the Winter, time to sharpen and shake the cobwebs from our tools and start working in the fields. In many traditions, especially in the colder parts of the world, this is among the most celebrated periods of the whole calendar.

Two thousand years ago, Spring began at 0° Aries, where the zodiac constellation of Aries was, physically. Now, however, the Spring Equinox occurs in the constellation of Pisces due to the Precession of the Equinoxes. This is caused in part by the Earth's wobble and the motion of the Sun about its celestial centre.

By fixing the first degree of Aries at the exact moment the Sun crosses the Equator, Hipparchus fixed the Tropical Zodiac (our astrological system) to the Spring Equinox. He made it easier for astrologers and astronomers to calculate the first day of Spring, long before computers. This is why many people consider that the Precession of the Equinoxes through the zodiac explains the great ages humanity has been through.

For instance, they identify the Age of Pisces with the age of Jesus and Christianity, chivalry and the elevation of womanhood. Others would argue that nothing has changed, men still hold the balance of power, people are still starving and are killed in vicious wars. Perhaps the Age of Aquarius will be different.

The Vernal or Spring Equinox and the Autumnal Equinox - when the Sun crosses the Equator

When the Sun crosses the Equator, this marks the beginning of activity in the direction the Sun moves. If it is heading North, then the Northern Hemisphere awakens to Spring, while the Southern Hemisphere heads into Autumn. Accordingly, they are named the Spring or Vernal Equinox (Northern Hemisphere) and the Autumnal Equinox (Southern Hemisphere). This corresponds to the zodiac Signs for Spring and Autumn - the Northern Spring Equinox in April falls at 0° Aries, while the Autumnal Equinox in September falls at 0° Libra.

The Summer Solstice and the Winter Solstice - also known as Midsummer and Midwinter, the moment the Sun reaches the Tropic of Cancer and Tropic of Capricorn

When the Sun travels to its furthest position North, as far as it can possibly go, it represents the Northern Hemisphere's 'Mid Summer's Day' or 'Mid Summer's Eve'. This is also called the Summer Solstice and occurs in the month of June. When the Sun is at its lowest in the northern sky in December, it is known as 'Mid Winter's Day' or 'Mid Winter's Eve'. This is true for the Northern Hemisphere, and it is the other way around in the Southern Hemisphere.

The Natal Chart - orientation

The natal chart lies flat on a sheet of paper and is drawn to physically represent the position of the Planets in their zodiac Signs or constellations, all 12 of them (not the 88 that are recognised by astronomers). We are Tropical astrologers and we know that the Planets are not exactly in the same Signs as for the Sidereal or Hindu astrologers. We accept that the Signs are fixed in the Tropical Zodiac at exactly 30°.

When we look at the chart, we first need to orient the Sun and the Planets to a day/night point. We do this by using the exact moment of birth, the date, and the geographic longitude and latitude of the native's place of birth. After this, we can 'fix' or draw up the natal chart and start to interpret it.

Using professional astronomical tables (ephemeris) of the planetary positions, or much easier, a computer, the birth time gives us the exact degree upon which the Eastern Horizon points to a Tropical zodiac Sign.

For example, if you were born exactly at dawn, the Sun will sit right on the horizon. In the natal chart your Sun will be at the exact degree of the Sign on the Eastern Horizon point. This Eastern Horizon point is called the **Ascendant or Rising** Sign.

This means that at the exact moment of your birth, the Eastern horizon was pointing at your Ascending or Rising Sign. For instance, if your Eastern Horizon is at 29° Capricorn, then we would say that you have Capricorn Rising, or you have a Capricorn Ascendant.

From this calculation we can determine what zodiac Sign was directly above you in the sky at the exact moment of your birth, this is called your **Midheaven.**

It is absolutely essential to calculate these two points of the Horoscope or Natal chart in both Sidereal and Tropical astrology. It allows us to calculate the Houses (House Cusps) and begin an accurate delineation or interpretation of the chart.

Point to Remember: the Planets travel in an anti-clockwise direction around the horoscope while the outer circle of the zodiac Signs travel 1° for each 4 minutes of time, in a clockwise direction. Don't stress, it does get easier as you go. At first, I was also frustrated when I had to remember everything, but it got a lot easier with practice.

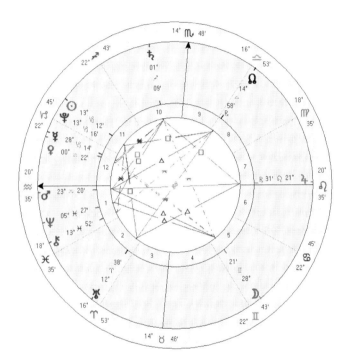

Pluto's Cave
Natal Chart
4 Jan 2015, Sun
9:00 am AEDT -11:00
canberra, Australia
35°S17'149°E08'
Geocentric
Tropical
Koch
True Node

23

How to Read the Chart

If you look at the top left corner, you will see the name, the date and time of birth (with the regional code and + or - hours from the Greenwich Meridian in England), and the place of birth and its geographic longitude and latitude. These features are critical when creating an accurate natal chart.

Every horoscope also has a description that informs you that it is Geocentric (from an Earth perspective), Tropical (uses the Western House system), Placidus (Placidus House system), True Node (not the mean or average of the North Node), Rating AA (the Rodden rating system that tells us how accurate a birth time is, AA means it is from a reliable source).

The charts in this book are just perfect for this task. I know next to nothing about these four people, this is why I decided to use them for this purpose.

There is one important point I would like you to note: I am Australian. As such, I have never followed, studied or had any interest in American politics. A lot of my readers may hold very strong opinions for and/or against the two politicians I have chosen for our guest charts. I picked them because they are powerful people with powerful charts and I will interpret them as if they were my clients. Again, I have zero interest in American politics, please keep that in mind when you read my comments. Whatever your opinion of these people, please do not take my descriptions personally.

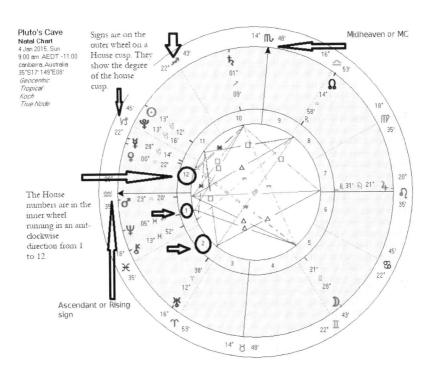

Pluto's Cave
Natal Chart
4 Jan 2015, Sun
9:00 am AEDT -11:00
canberra, Australia
35°S17' 149°E08'
Geocentric
Tropical
Koch
True Node

Signs are on the outer wheel on a House cusp. They show the degree of the house cusp.

Midheaven or MC

The House numbers are in the inner wheel running in an anti-clockwise direction from 1 to 12.

Ascendant or Rising sign

25

Meditating with the Astrological Archetypes

There is a very powerful way to understand astrology and to know yourself at the deepest level of your being: through meditation. Inscribed on the forecourt of the Temple of Apollo at Delphi, are the words, "**Know Thyself**". It aptly describes what it is that astrology and psychology together can help you do. If you are unsure or uncomfortable, you can seek out a trained therapist to guide you through these meditation exercises.

Your 1st House Cusp Sign is your Ascendant and this is where you begin your inner quest to 'Know Thyself'.

May I suggest that you first go online or get a few books and look at a few artistic illustrations of the Signs of the zodiac. Begin by building some imagery around the various Signs so that you have something to focus on when you start meditating.

In tarot there are many decks and pictures to choose from, but in astrology we have to rely on our imagination and abstract symbols. Don't worry about this, the longer and deeper you work with your archetypes, the more you will develop your own, unique set of images for them. Look how they appear in my meditations, many are not what you would normally expect.

'Practice makes perfect', the saying is old but true. The more dedicated your practice, the more perfect your outcomes, especially in meditation.

If you can, close your eyes and imagine yourself facing your Ascendant Sign. You can try with your eyes open, but I find this can be distracting. Imagine looking at your Ascendant standing or sitting right there on your chart, or walking with you on a beach, or in a cafe sipping a cup of hot chocolate with you… the imagery available to you is infinite, you don't need to impose limits.

Engage your senses as much as possible, smells, tastes, sounds, feelings, sense of touch, visual clues, colours, shapes, sizes, patterns, textures, warmth, etc. With exercise you will get better and better.

Not everyone can close their eyes and see a panorama with full colour, not all can interact with their inner world straight away, it generally takes practice, lots of it. Yet I find that most people can do it in one sitting if they have a guide to help them - this is your guide.

When I gave presentations on using the natal chart in meditation and self development, I would lay out a wheel of cord on the floor in 12 segments, just like the chart itself. I would then place people around it to represent the Planets, the House Cusps and the Signs. The person the chart represented would then stand in the middle of the 'chart' picturing themselves as actually standing inside their horoscope, in trance.

Introducing My Meditations

To help you get started, I decided to demonstrate how I work with a natal chart as a psychotherapist. I will keep this personal and use my own chart for this purpose: each meditation is about me. While it can be embarrassing at times, I do think you need the most honest description possible to understand the process.

I have been meditating for many years as part of my practice of tai chi and soon began to astral travel almost every night. This is how I set out to explore the secrets that lay beyond consciousness, a journey I embarked on some 30 years ago. In fact, this is why I went back to university and became a psychologist.

During my long years of clinical hypnotherapy practice, I have developed and refined this style of meditation as a therapeutic technique for those interested in taking the spiritual path. When I took people into their natal chart in a light trance state, it proved quite simple and very effective at the same time. Direct work with the astrological archetypes frequently led to extremely useful insights, and it boosted psychological healing.

I don't want to give the impression that this is easy or that everyone will want to do this type of psychotherapy or meditation. Those who tried it improved considerably, many still continue with their archetypal meditations at home.

The meditations I share with you in this book demonstrate how I connect and engage with my own astrological archetypes. If you choose to follow this method, your insights and experiences will probably be quite different from mine. You will notice that these meditations are 'therapeutic'; they provide insight normally gained in a psychotherapy session.

The material I share with you here was not at all easy to record. I discovered many years ago that I needed to go into deep trance before I could connect with my archetypes. As a consequence, sometimes I would fall asleep and forget what happened next. In those particular instances I would go back into trance to repeat it all over again. Sometimes it took three or four meditations to make sure that I had fully experienced what the archetypes wanted me to learn and record.

Some meditations flowed easily, they were short and easy to interpret, while others took a lot of time and effort. This is very personal material, the archetypes did not pull their punches and I don't share this with you lightly. The archetypes were honest and fully focused on my desire to demonstrate how I interact with them. My intention is to make this information available to you for your benefit as a student of psychological astrology.

I hope they help illustrate that you can also connect intimately with your astrological archetypes. You don't need anything special, just a quiet place to sit or lie down and then imagine standing in the middle of your chart. They won't bite you!

Please feel free to contact me and share your experiences.

The Twelve Houses of the Horoscope
Calculating House Cusps

As you have noticed, each natal chart is divided into 12 sectors. These are called the Houses, and the line separating them is called the House Cusp, or just Cusp. This always has a zodiac Sign sitting on it. For instance in Barack Obama's chart, Scorpio is the zodiac Sign on the Cusp of his 10th House. This is also called the Midheaven or MC - thus he has a Scorpio Midheaven.

Some astrologers do not work with Houses (like Cosmobiologists) but all astrologers use the birth time to determine your Ascendant and your Midheaven.

Most western practitioners use the Placidus House System which was created by the monk Placidus (1603 - 1668). He was the first astronomer / astrologer to create a set of tables that allowed both beginners and experts to create their own proper horoscope, with accurate House Cusps. Prior to his contribution, it was almost impossible to erect your own horoscope. House Cusps and the accurate positions of the Planets in the zodiac Signs required such complicated calculations only astronomers and mathematicians could create a horoscope.

You can imagine that three hundred years ago a set of tables that allowed you to draw up your own astrological charts was worth a king's ransom. Today, we use computers and have no idea why the Planets, Houses and Signs are where they are. This is not a disadvantage, as long as we know how to interpret what we get and how to correct it when something is wrong. I learned how to calculate House Cusps and the positions of the Planets to the exact degree by hand, and it was murder. A single miscalculation would render the chart useless. I really prefer my computer these days.

There are many ways to calculate the House Cusps, but Placidus is the most common. Each House System is man-made, they do not come from the Planets, from the sky or the stars themselves. The Placidus House System works best for birth places close to the Equator. For those born closer to the poles, the Houses begin to squeeze together and become extremely large or extremely small. At the Equator, the Houses are equal in size.

Other astrologers have created their own system to lessen the distortion of Houses due to longitude. Personally, I prefer Koch which works slightly better in extreme latitudes, but Placidus is still a popular choice for many.

As you explore and practice your astrology readings, you will eventually choose your own House system. I use Placidus in this book and in my courses because it has been around for ages and is widely used by astrologers all over the world.

Point to Remember: all House Cusps form a continuous line, opposite House Cusps have the same degree and minute. For instance in Barack Obama's chart, Pisces is at 18° and 03' on the 2nd House Cusp. This means that its opposite Sign, Virgo, is on the opposing House Cusp, the 8th, at exactly the same degree and minute, 18° 03'.

The House Cusps

Each Planet is in charge of a Sign, and by correspondence, it rules the House attached to that Sign. Any Planet in that House also contributes to the meaning and interpretation of that House. It is the Sign on the House Cusp that informs us as to which Planet rules the affairs of that House.

All the charts in this book use the Placidus House System, to keep it simple. Therefore, Houses will come in various sizes. I sometimes use the Koch House system if the Houses become unmanageable, but I will not do that in this book.

When looking at the charts in this lesson, note how the birth time and the geographic longitude and latitude changes the shape of the chart. Planets, House Cusps and their Signs are all placed differently. They will have an impact on how you interpret the chart.

For more information on Rulerships, please go to the Appendix and view the grids. I am not going to expand on planetary Rulerships at this stage, as it is beyond the scope of this book.

Point to Remember: the Cusp of a House is very important, it receives emphasis when a Planet approaches in Transit, or if it lies within an orb of 8° natally. For instance, if Mars is sitting within 8° of the Ascendant, this makes Mars more powerful and its qualities will flow into the first House itself.

The Ascendant and The Midheaven

The Ascendant or Rising Sign is the Cusp of the 1st House. This translates as the Sign that is Ascending (or Rising) on the eastern horizon at the moment of your birth.

The Signs of the zodiac pass across the eastern horizon (Ascendant) at roughly 1° every four minutes. This is due to the rotation of the Earth spinning about its axis. The Ascendant, therefore, points to a different degree of a Sign every 4 minutes. This can mean the difference between an Aquarius Rising at 29° and a Pisces Rising at 0° - just a few minutes can change your Ascendant Sign.

The First House Cusp is ALWAYS called the Ascendant or Rising Sign. This is your Ego and what you are prepared to give of yourself to the world. It shows what you think of yourself, how self-confident you are and how you interact with others. It is also your physical body. Your 1st House Cusp, your Ascendant, can also indicate your constitutional health, vulnerabilities and physical ailments.

It represents a large facet of your personality and is known as the 'mask' you wear in front of strangers, workmates, when in company etc. The mask is a Jungian description which describes the role of the Ascendant quite well.

Your Midheaven is on the Cusp of the 10th House, it is so called because it is at the middle of the Heavens, and Heaven is always above us. Simply put, your Midheaven is the Sign directly above you at the moment of your birth. The Sign on the Cusp of the 10th House, or Midheaven, is very important: it represents your direction in life, what you strive to achieve, what you are reaching for and your chances of success.

These two are the most important House Cusps of your chart. As a psychologist, this is where I begin to pick up my first impressions of your personality.

The Ascendant and Midheaven of our four guest charts

Barack Obama - his Ascendant is Aquarius, his Midheaven is Scorpio, his Sun is in Leo in the 6th House and his Moon is in Gemini in the 4th.

Hilary Clinton - her Ascendant is Scorpio and her Midheaven is Virgo, her Sun is in Scorpio in the 12th House and her Moon is in Pisces in the 4th.

Justin Bieber - his Ascendant is in Scorpio, his Midheaven is in Virgo, his Sun is in Pisces in the 3rd House and his Moon is in Libra in the 11th.

Taylor Swift is interesting, she has two birth times. This is a perfect opportunity to explore just how important an accurate birth time really is. Chart 1 gives us her **Facebook birth time.** This is the time she gave on her Facebook page. It shows 8:36 a.m., a mid-morning birth. According to the **Facebook time,** she has a Capricorn Ascendant and Scorpio Midheaven, her Sun is in Sagittarius in the 12th House and her Moon is in Cancer in the 6th.

But, hold on a second, she had **Twittered a different birth time**, which is nearly 12 hours later, 8:46 p.m., in the evening. Her **Twittered chart** shows completely different Houses. Her new Ascendant is Leo, her Midheaven is now Taurus, her Sun has moved 1/2 a degree further in this 12-hour period and it is in the 5th House, and her Moon has moved even further, from 3° to 10° of Cancer and is now in the 11th House. Her chart has moved almost 180°.

Which one is her correct birth time? The one on Facebook or on Twitter? 8:36 a.m. or 8:46 p.m.?

Please note how her House sizes are changed by this 12 hour difference: her **Facebook time** has the 1st, 2nd, 7th and 8th as the largest Houses, but for the **Twittered time** it is her 3rd, 4th, 9th and 10th Houses that are the biggest in size.

When we look at the Midheaven, it appears as if the chart has twisted around too. It is important to notice that each Planet is now in a different House. This will make a huge difference in our interpretation of her personality.

A Planet in a Sign in a House says everything about the person. If we move one component, its House placement, we get a completely different reading. That's what an incorrect birth time will do, alter the chart and change your reading.

Empty Houses

It is very common to find some Houses that do not contain any Planets. This is called an 'Empty House'. Although it may be empty it does not diminish the power of that House. When a House is empty we use the House cusp Sign to locate its Planetary Rulership. You will find the Rulerships grid at the end of this book.

To give an example, Barack Obama's 10th House does not contain any Planets. However, Scorpio is the Sign on its cusp and Pluto rules Scorpio. Pluto, as the ruler of Scorpio, will pull or draw the 10th House into the House where he resides. We can see that Pluto resides in Barack's 7th House. The 7th House now contains Pluto, North Node and Uranus, and it also contains the entire 10th House.

To understand the 10th House we must also understand it in terms of its rulership by Pluto, the House where Pluto resides and any aspects to Pluto himself. Delineating rulerships and its impact on the Houses themselves is an advanced technique which will be discussed in another book.

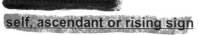

self, ascendant or rising sign

This is the House of the skin, it is what you touch the world with, your physical, emotional and spiritual skin so to speak. It can also become thickened armour to protect your sensitive Self, your inner weaknesses are hidden within the shell of your Ascendant.

To use an allegory from the animal kingdom, this armour can manifest as aggressiveness, assertiveness, leadership or as condescending behaviour. It can be a dog with its tail between its legs. Or it can be a dog with its head held high with pride because it's been treated with respect and knows its own worth. Or one that is smart and self-confident, trying to prove its worth in the world of dogs. Your first House is where you connect with the world around you.

It is therefore your initial unconscious, impulsive reaction when you are confronted with life events. It shows how you react instinctively and without thought. It is also freedom, the freedom from restraint of a baby forced into this world. It can also indicate your birth experience.

I will relate my own birth experience. I have a Capricorn Ascendant, and just 3° away, in the first House, sits Chiron, the Wounded Healer. My mother told me that it took her three days to give birth to me. Each time she went into labour it would stop. I never gave this much thought, I just didn't want to enter this crazy world, who would?

In my late 20's, I tried a new-age therapy called Rebirthing. I lay on the soft futon, practiced cyclic breathing and went into my unconscious. I found myself holding onto and wrestling with cold steel prison bars. I wanted to get out desperately. I was being squashed. I could feel the contractions squeezing the life out of me. I had to get out, immediately! I felt overheated from the exertion of trying to get through those bars.

My life was being crushed by the contractions. I was very hot, frustrated, I almost panicked, desperate to escape. I knew that I was fighting for my life, if I stayed there, I would die.

That birth experience stayed with me, unconsciously, inside my body, so well hidden that I had no idea it was there. Whenever I felt trapped or had to physically struggle, I would become frustrated, hot, panicky and I would force my way through this invisible barrier to get to the other side regardless of the consequences.

It felt like a matter of life and death. Maybe this is why I have always been so determined to continue to transcend consciousness, to go beyond this physical existence. This is why I take others into their inner world too, beyond consciousness, because I nearly died at childbirth. It is just a theory, but it fits my loaded and powerful 8th House.

One side of Capricorn is his ability to restrain, frustrate, hold back, limit and build tension, this was my birth experience. Chiron has been my teacher, he insisted that this was my wound, I had to experience it, learn from it and use this knowledge to help others. Chiron reveals how close I was to dying, his gift was my psychological wound, and my desire to transcend consciousness.

Most commonly, the 1st House is what you show to the world, it is the 'mask' you wear to protect yourself. If you look at your natal chart as your physical representation, your Ascendant corresponds to what you present at the very start - your first physical and psychological impression on others.

It is the sunrise that unveils all that was hidden and what you are prepared to show the world from the shadows lurking within..

Psychologically, the first House is the outer assemblage of your fears, lusts, desires and emotional needs. You either project it on others in your quest to get what you need from life or it is projected on objects, work and play.

Projection is commonly seen in the 7th House, the House of love, romance, clients, customers and very close relationships. It is in the light of the Descendant (exactly opposite the Ascendant) that it becomes visible. It will be obvious in your relationships and how you interact with others.

Sometimes we can 'see' another person's Ascendant because it is what they show us most clearly. It is what they want us to notice and what they like us to believe they are like. Once you know them very well, the person will let you see more of their inner Self.

A concentration of Planets in the first House shows that the native is focused on or driven to experience life as an adventure. Perhaps they come across as instinctively impulsive and hyperactive mentally, as well as physically - risk taking is a common trait. Freedom is thoroughly appreciated by a person with a loaded 1st House.

Archetypal Meditation - Ascendant and 1st House

My Meditation: *in preparation for this chapter, I decided to get in touch with my Ascendant, Capricorn. He was very tall and had extremely long arms and an elongated face. He was thin and angular, pretty much as is described in most astrology books. He was really nice though, the typical gentle giant. I liked him immediately and I wanted to nurture him. What a funny thought, me nurturing an archetype, but he brought out qualities in me that I would never have associated with solid, steadfast and disciplined Capricorn.*

He didn't say much, in fact I have forgotten what we talked about because I fell asleep soon after our chat and I can't remember, sorry about that. However, I did get the impression after I woke up that he was very comfortable as my Ascendant. It is a huge responsibility to be the Sign ruled by Saturn, **the Lord of the Chart.** *Capricorn takes this responsibility very seriously.*

Capricorn gave me the impression that he had no aggression at all, he actually avoided conflict. I even witnessed him demonstrate this during my meditation. Just below him sits Chiron, about 3° from the Cusp of the 1st House, very close.

They stand almost side by side, so I guess they have to get along, otherwise how painful would that be, years and years being stuck there together with nothing to talk about. For some reason, Chiron was going on about something to do with spiritual growth. Capricorn must have heard it before because he just got up and walked away. Aha, hey, that's what I feel like doing sometimes when I don't want to tell someone that they are boring me.

I found the qualities of Capricorn stifling in my teens and when I was a young adult, I felt he held me back. It was not so, I later realised that he actually held me together.

In some of my newsletters I have described a series of meditations that helped me cope with a very difficult period in my life. On those occasions, I did not see a human figure at all, Capricorn was a mountain. It was cut in half by a muddy river: this was Neptune transiting my Ascendant.

I can sometimes see Capricorn in his goat form climbing that mountain. Yes, it is still there with a beautiful life-giving river flowing below it. Again, before writing this section, Capricorn invited me to ride on his back down the mountain. It was terrifying, seriously frightening but exhilarating at the same time.

This is my meditation to give you a concrete example of what I am trying to describe. I don't expect anyone else to go through something exactly like this. Each meditation with an archetype is individual, unique to your own psyche. I suggest that you practice these House Cusp meditations every day. You are sure to gain valuable insights that will benefit your spiritual growth as well as help with your astrological practice.

Interpreting the Ascendant – please view the guest charts in the Appendix at the end of the book

Barack Obama - has an Aquarian Ascendant which suggests that he is adventurous, intelligent and humanitarian, particularly as he presents himself in public. Aquarius Rising shows that Obama likes to be seen by others as interesting, inspired, intellectual, sharp, intuitive, inventive and caring. He also has Chiron, the Wounded Healer, in his first House. This Planet indicates that he has a fundamental wound, be it physical or psychological, but it is there. This gives him compassion and empathy that touches others. As they say, the best healer is someone with the same injury. Interestingly, this First House adds depth and personality in a big way: it is generally the first thing you notice about a person.

Hilary Clinton - has a Scorpio Ascendant, showing that she is intense, sexually attractive, passionate and commanding. This is one heck of a powerful lady. Scorpio is the Sign of transformation and crisis, she must first undergo many crises to grow as a person, and Hilary has been through the fire of Hades to get where she is today. Without going into details here, those four Planets in her 12th House deserve attention, make note of them when you read her 12th House. Hilary has Jupiter in her first House contributing to her powerful and charismatic aura. Like Obama's Chiron, Jupiter has a strong influence in her life, it is jovial, fun loving, expansive and it rules law, morals and justice. Hilary has a strong and powerful ally in Jupiter.

Justin Bieber - also has a Scorpio Ascendant and he has three Planets in his 12th House. Scorpio is spirited and sensitive. It tends to grow through critical situations as we saw with Hilary, but it manifests differently than in her case. Justin is an artist, a performer, and music is his life - though drugs seem to have taken centre stage lately. We could say that Justin likes to call the shots himself, he will not let anyone take charge of his life. Scorpio wants to control, it is safer this way than someone else controlling him. The sensitivity of Scorpio needs him to run the show so he doesn't become emotionally overwhelmed.

Taylor Swift Facebook Time - I will use her Facebook birth time with the Capricorn Ascendant and then compare it with her Twitter birth time. Her Facebook time shows a very busy 1st House indeed, hyperactive and impulsive. She has five Planets: Mercury, Neptune, Saturn, Venus and the North Node in her 1st House. This adds a lot of energy to her creativity and her presentation on stage. Her need to express herself with that large stellium in her 1st House is heavily impacted by Capricorn's need to structure and hide everything. A Capricorn Ascendant is generally quite shy, you don't see behind their strong Mask, they are careful to the extreme.

Taylor Swift Twitter Time - Leo Ascendant: outgoing, generous, gregarious and charming, the Sun shines from her and everyone loves her. She shows great creativity, her stage presence is impressive and she can reach everyone's heart through her songs. She has no Planets in the 1st House, but that doesn't really matter at this stage. I will explain more later, as we get deeper in the charts.

Point to Remember: each degree is made up of 60' (minutes), 60' = 1°. There are 30° in one zodiac Sign. Houses are not fixed; their size varies according to many factors.

1st House Planetary Ruler	Mars
Sign Correspondence	Aries
Angles/Qualities	Angular
Elements / Trinities	Fire / Life
Health	The head and face, the five senses
Keywords	appearance, early childhood years, presentation, ego, personality, vitality, health in general, the mask, self. From your reading add your own key-words to these lists

The first house is similar
to rising. It is the guard
you put up for others
you arent close to. If you
have many placements in
the first house you are
closed off and dont easily
open up. the signs in your
first house are how you
want to be seen by other
people

The Second House

security

This is the House of security and all it encompasses: material security in terms of finances, your income and how you make money. It also represents your possessions. It is about spiritual security: your beliefs, values and attitudes, as well as your emotional safety in terms of anxiety and apprehension. It is also your attitude to making money and to the stability it brings. Financial, material, psychological and spiritual security is shown through this House. Psychologically, it can show whether the native is prone to emotional insecurity.

The 2nd House, the Sign on its Cusp and its planetary ruler will help you understand how the native handles personal insecurity, physical assault, fear of abandonment. It also shows personal bankruptcy and how they deal with money, whether they are cautious or careless.

For instance, Pisces on the 2nd House Cusp can help explain why the native never has any money: they have little interest in or concept of how to manage their finances. Someone with Taurus on this Cusp would be more cautious with material possessions and money in general. They can often fill whole rooms, garages and any spare space with old and useless belongings from around the neighbourhood, or from their childhood.

Some astrologers liken the 2nd House to the 8th, saying that it also represents the psychological aspects of security, and insecurity. In that case it becomes a suitable House to examine the psychological impact of the native's need to feel safe. Some people have enormous demands for grandeur, money, power, sex, success, love or even spiritual fulfillment. These can all be placed in the 2nd House of material, psychological, emotional and spiritual needs.

This House also corresponds to Taurus, and if we examine the Taurean traits, we can better understand this House of security. Taureans like feeling safe, and particularly enjoy physical comforts. They like to make sure that they have two of everything just in case one breaks, that the bed is warm before they jump in and their food is cooked to their requirements - they will sulk if its isn't.

People with a strong 2nd House know the value of a well prepared house for sale, they get the vibe of what other people need for comfort. They know about home security because they have such a strong need for it themselves.

Most of us don't have the Sun in Taurus or in the 2nd House, so how do the rest of us who aren't Taureans, understand these 2nd House / Taurean traits and qualities?

We all experience security on many levels, it is how we survive. It is very difficult to feel safe emotionally when you are about to lose your job or your home. Therefore the 2nd House is best understood as linked to our immediate security needs. If we feel safe now, we can find ways to deal with any challenge.

For some people, when they lose their possessions, it can affect them at a soul level. If you have a strong 4th, 8th or 12th House, this becomes a personal crisis that pervades your entire being.

Second House material security issues can lead to 8th House climaxes. The 8th House existential crisis can only be triggered if it is already just below the surface. The 2nd House can provoke it, but the predisposition must be there first.

People with a dominance of Planets in their 2nd House are drawn to seek security. On the material level, this could manifest as buying a new gadget, like a lawn mower. On the physical level, it could be craving for a home-made Italian pizza. On the psychological side, maybe you'd long for a cuddle before going to bed. And on the spiritual plane, you might feel the need to go to church each Sunday - plus Bible study twice a week, just in case.

A strong 2nd House, a stellium of three or more Planets, can generally survive a security crisis. They may throw tantrums and get upset but they turn around and rebuild themselves. If these Planets are poorly aspected, however, they could swing the other way and focus attention on the negative aspects of this House.

If a 2nd House person loses everything they have, they will generally recover. But if they have insecurities lying deep within their unconscious, it could lead to a psychological crisis. The first is a 2nd House quality, the second one belongs in the 8th or 12th House.

Archetypal Meditation - 2nd House

All you need to do is follow the same exercise as for your Ascendant meditation. Please make sure you record all your astrological meditations, they can help guide you in your spiritual quest.

My Meditation: *I have Aquarius on my 2nd House Cusp, the Water bearer, she is so sweet, but She is also a He and He is quite hyperactive. He is exciting so I don't really mind his strange and eccentric ways.*

When she is the Water Bearer she is calm and serene. It's a sweetness that comes from compassion, caring and wanting the best for others. She is so Greek, when she walks out of her Cusp in my meditation she has a flowing white silk gown, extremely feminine. It is a sharp contrast to her male side, he is the eccentric, muddle-headed scientist who tries to solve the problems of the world in an instant.

The scientist is like Doctor Emmett Brown from the 'Back To The Future' movies. He is seriously busy and doesn't keep in touch with me too often. The two work together though: she provides the nourishment as the Water Bearer and he has the task of bringing it to my psyche. Hmm, that's interesting.

A bi-gendered archetype? I actually prefer it this way. I get two archetypes instead of one. I wonder if anyone else has a double sided Aquarius archetype?

I don't use these archetypes very much in my inner work, they seem to be quite content doing their thing. I suppose that now that I have become more conscious of them, we might work together more in the future.

This was not a deep and meaningful meditation, it was more of an introduction, I have never met the mad scientist before. He is ruled by

Uranus on my 7th House Cusp which we will discuss later on. It's Uranus that I often work with rather than the 2nd House. Looks like I can add another meditation to my 'to do' list.

Chart Interpretations:

Barack Obama - has Pisces on his 2nd Cusp, this shows that he is not the least interested in material things, he is probably quite relaxed about this aspect of life. He may, however, become stressed quite easily and needs emotional, rather than material security. Feeling safe is anchored to spiritual and emotional needs rather than material ones.

Hilary Clinton - Sagittarius is on her 2nd House Cusp, this suggests that she would pursue material wealth as if setting out on an adventure. Money comes to her easily and she enjoys both making and spending it: she is carefree. Sagittarius is the Sign of adventure and irresponsibility, she could even get into deep waters with this Sign placement on the 2nd House Cusp. However, I am sure there are other Planets and Signs that mitigate this and make her less compulsive and irresponsible security-wise.

Justin Bieber - Capricorn is on his 2nd House Cusp suggesting that he keeps his money under guard, maybe even buried under his House. If there ever was a Sign of the zodiac that hoards money and possessions, it's Capricorn, and sometimes Taurus, as well. Capricorn is cautious, way more cautious than Taurus. That means thinking ahead for a rainy day, for a whole rainy month, just in case.

Taylor Swift Facebook Time - Aquarius sits on her 2nd House of security suggesting that money comes and goes, sometimes it abounds and sometimes it doesn't. Aquarius isn't particularly interested in security as such, but it loves spending, for sure. This Sign can also suggest that she will stress and worry if her bank account is not full to the brim.

Taylor Swift Twitter Time - Virgo on the 2nd House Cusp is a Sign that is careful with money and possessions, as well as with feelings and other people's finances. Virgo here is a very wise Sign for security, always thinking and considering opportunities to spare money and be safe materially, physically, emotionally and spiritually.

2nd House Planetary Ruler	Venus (Passive)
Sign Correspondence	Taurus
Angles/Qualities	Succedent
Elements / Trinities	Earth / Wealth
Health	The neck and throat
Keywords	money, security, safety, material possessions, earning ability, values, beliefs, ability to support others, anxiety due to emotional insecurity

The second House is that of comfort
and security. whether its on a physical
(material possetions) emotional (needy,
constant) or spiritual (community)
level, If you have a dominant
second house, you crave comfort,
homklyness and routine.

The Third House

communication

This House shows how the native communicates and also illustrates some more negative mental activities associated with this House, like nervousness or an overactive mind. It represents their schooling and how they handled the stress and opportunities of their education. It also represents how they communicate, how they handle small talk at the office, their socialising, routines and habits, whether they are skilled speakers and commentators, how they learn in general. It is the House of the conscious mind.

Travel is often seen in this House but it is only the short trips from work to home, etc. as part of their daily routine. It also shows how they relate to electrical appliances, siblings and neighbours. A person with Sagittarius on this Cusp would have good relations with their brothers and sisters but would often forget them in the rush to find another adventure. They would get bored at school and need constant activity and inspiration to learn.

This House is very useful in my personal practice. It is highly informative if someone has a stellium or mini stellium here - especially when the personal or Inner Planets are involved. I would interpret that as possible irritability, excessive worry, stress, negative self-talk, nasty thoughts.

When someone has a stellium or some other planetary focus on this House I always recommend that they learn to relax their mind. I give them my self hypnosis CD to practice at least once a day and go back to it before turning in for the night. This is also the House emphasized in the chart of the guy next door who prefers doing night shifts. Insomnia, disturbed sleep and mental activity that is simply too much to let you fall asleep can be seen in this House, and during therapy sessions.

I sometimes recommend physical activity like jogging, walking, tai chi, yoga, gym, etc. to people with a strong 3rd House to help them unwind mentally. Physical exercise does them a world of good, they can get out of their head and into their body.

Many people live inside their head. Yes, it's true that when you have persistent pain from an injury or chronic anxiety or depression, you tend to avoid going into your body because that's where it hurts. We call them 'feelings' because we feel them in our body. Have you ever had a broken heart? Then you know what I mean.

These natives respond particularly well to progressive relaxation exercises like self-hypnosis, or a meditation style that walks them through every part of their body until they are relaxed. Getting these 3rd House people out of their heads and into their bodies is a very efficient therapy. It helps them get some sleep too.

Archetypal Meditation - 3rd House Archetype meditations

My Meditation: I have Pisces on my 3rd House Cusp, no wonder I struggled through school with my head in the clouds, I felt quite lost and spent most of my time on my own. I was certainly bright enough, but I was usually somewhere else. My head was filled with music, songs and poems I wrote many years before. At school, I felt like a rabbit caught in the headlights of a car, I had no choice but to endure it.

It's a struggle to write clearly, words just swim around in my head and I can't always get them in order. You probably already noticed my writing style, it's so much easier if I write the way I talk. Can you imagine how hard it was at university, and twice? When I was teaching, I always had to have a dictionary on me. Words are music, they carry a message in sound and flow, pitch and rhyme, they float. If I try and formulate them into a logical sentence on a page they will just swim around playfully in my head. It takes me ages if I want to discipline them and write them down.

Pisces is ruled by Neptune, and Neptune sits right at the top of my chart, just inside my 10th House. He is conjunct my Midheaven (10th House Cusp). Neptune is the **Planet of High Degree,** he shines his light over my entire chart, like a lamp post in the night illuminating everything nearby. My psyche is infused with Neptunian energy, my Pisces 3rd House Cusp is bathing in it, too.

I am in the ocean and walking along the bottom of the sea. I can breath, it's easy. King Neptune with his trident and a merman's tail swims over to greet me and ushers me into his cave. He looks like a cartoon character, I hear bubbles, maybe too much TV, or Disney's 'The Little Mermaid?

There is a treasure chest overflowing with jewels and gold coins just inside the cave. I know it represents his gifts to me, but what I really want instead is to ride that shark swimming next to us.

I become the shark and can feel his joy as he revels in his enormous power. Swimming is power and the water is power to. It's not very clear, but it doesn't matter.

I am afraid of the deep sea, it's fun to splash around in the shallows but further out where I cannot see the bottom, eeek! The shark-me, however, just floats untroubled in the calm waters, in the middle of nowhere. I can't see much further than about 10 meters or so, because the water is a cloud of turquoise particles. I am floating, no movement, just floating in stillness amongst the particles.

I feel a little fearful, my mind is racing with worry about being eaten by some hidden creature from the deep. I am afraid because I don't know what is around me. Then I remember that I am a shark and I rule the oceans, I am nobody's dinner.

We dwell in the same spot for ages, my mind begins to calm down at last. The shark says, "Don't look, feel." But I do look, and the ocean is an endless expanse of nothingness below me. I am becoming upset again, what if some monster comes for me, from those dark depths. "Close your eyes and feel," says the shark matter-of-factly.

I focus on my sense of Feeling, and something unexpected happens. I hear a sound, more sounds, blends, harmonies, WHALES! A family of whales appears out of the gloom surging towards me, I dissolve out of the shark into one of the whales. "Now this is real power!" says the whale delightedly. I am excited too, I am so happy, I feel so powerful. I feel their songs in my body, I sing with them, the vibrations through my chest almost overwhelm me.

Wealth: the whale sends me an image of the treasure chest in

Neptune's cave. "This is the treasure!" he says to me. I have passed another test. Indeed this is a real treasure, I smile to myself. Now I understand. Whenever I am in the ocean, or in any deep water, I need to use my sense of Feeling. I need to take my time, slow things down, feel the water, the entire expanse of it. Just like the shark showed me, stay calm, don't think, don't rush, just feel it.

The other side to this treasure is to remain calm, focus on floating, not thinking. Thinking can lead to worry, so just feel, float and feel. The 3rd House is about thinking too much and worrying, so just be calm, feel. Yep, I get it now.

I will do some more whale meditations, they have such a deep understanding of life, not just about the oceans, but existence itself. It's difficult to explain.

I see Neptune in his cave smiling, I need to visit him again, it is not merely about Pisces, it is about Pisces AND Neptune. That makes me wonder why not a singular archetype… ahhh, but this is the very essence of what Pisces and Neptune represent. They blend, they flow through consciousness, they know no boundaries, they aren't singular at all, they are a fusion of energies. Like blending two colours, they mix to become one colour. It looks like I have more more meditation to do.

Chart Interpretations:

Barack Obama - has Taurus on his 3rd Cusp, although it is at 0°, so it could possibly be Aries at 29°. We need to keep in mind that a few minutes in birth time in either direction could impact the Sign on the Cusp when it is close to 30°. Taurus shows that he communicates in a careful and structured manner but also with passion and great articulation. This might show that his voice and physical presentation is strong and that he can express his emotions well to his audience. As a student, Obama would work hard and would be dedicated to his scholarly work. This is a solid placement for any mental activity.

Hilary Clinton - has Capricorn on her 3rd House Cusp suggesting that she is a very capable speaker who spends an enormous amount of time and energy preparing for every communication engagement. She would be a careful and dedicated student and is capable of making considered decisions. This, too, is a solid Sign placement for her mental activities.

Intercepted Sign - please note that within Hilary's 3rd House lies the Sign of Aquarius, try and find it on her outer wheel, it's missing. This doesn't mean it's really gone, only that Aquarius, fixed at exactly 30°, is too small to fit into this House. If you look at the Cusp degrees, you will see what I mean. The 3rd House Cusp is Capricorn at 28°, which leaves only 2° left in Capricorn. The 4th House Cusp is 5° Pisces, thus her 3rd House is 2° of Capricorn + 30° of Aquarius + 5° of Pisces = 37°. 37 is larger than 30 (the size of a Sign), so Aquarius fits in quite easily. We say that Aquarius is 'intercepted' in the 3rd House. This means that it is enclosed by the Signs on the Cusp of this House and the next. All we need to consider at this stage is that the intercepted Sign does not disappear from the chart, it is merely hidden in a large House.

Look at the House opposite the 3rd House Cusp, the 9th House Cusp. It is exactly the same size and the Sign of Leo is hidden or intercepted, too. That's how the Houses work, the Sign and degrees are exactly opposite each other.

Justin Bieber - has Aquarius on his 3rd House Cusp and it is quite loaded with a stellium, we would call this a '3rd House Stellium'. The Sign of Aquarius suggests that his mind takes leaps instead of processing information step by step like everybody else. His intellect is sharp, quick, but may be prone to stress and worry, insecurity and anxiety. It can also suggest disturbed sleep and difficulty falling asleep. This is something to look out for: when people turn to drugs and alcohol, they self-medicate to control their busy mind and get some rest. He is a restless thinker who probably experiences great bouts of creativity. He has the ability to come up with incredible word combinations.

Taylor Swift Facebook Time - Aries sits on her 3rd House Cusp suggesting that she may have been an active and aggressive chatterbox at school. With this placement, she may have been easily provoked to start arguments and probably fought a lot. It could have manifested as a great debater as well. It might also suggest that she is a sharp and intelligent young lady driven to succeed at all costs and works incredibly hard to achieve intellectual success.

Taylor Swift Twitter Time - the Sign on her 3rd House Cusp is Libra implying that she was quiet and peaceful at school, her voice would have developed through long hours of practice, singing to herself and to anyone who would listen. This is the Sign of compromise and so she would rarely stand up for herself at school, preferring to keep the peace. Intellectually, Libra is an Air Sign so she would not have had too much trouble learning.

3rd House Planetary Ruler	Mercury (Active)
Sign Correspondence	Gemini
Angles/Qualities	Cadent
Elements / Trinities	Air / Relationships
Health	The arms, hands, shoulders, fingers
Keywords	communications, siblings, socialisation, mental activity and conscious mind, intellectual pursuits, speaking skills, mental hobbies, quality of sleep, daydreaming or an acute and hyperactive mind

The Fourth House

Imum Coeli (IC), upbringing, childhood, house, home and family

This House is the first of our psychic or psychological Houses (4, 8, 12). It allows us to look into the person's psyche through their upbringing and family conditioning. Sigmund Freud helped us understand the importance of family and upbringing, which are the foundation of our instincts, needs and unconscious urges.

The 4th House indicates our father or our mother. Sometimes the father takes on the role of the mother in the family or vice versa, the mother is the dominant parent. I have had clients whose mother took on the role as the domineering aggressor.

Traditionally, the 4th House is ruled by the father while the 10th is ruled by the mother. However, Mother is represented by the Sign of Cancer, which is naturally on the 4th House Cusp, one would think that the 4th House should belong to the mother. Traditionalists say that the native's mother is better represented by the Myth of Capricorn. Amaltheia was the nymph-goat that saved Zeus (Jupiter) from his father Cronus (Saturn) who was in the habit of eating his children.

If we take this a step further, Capricorn is ruled by Saturn, discipline, order and structure, this is usually instilled by the father. I would associate this with the 10th House. For most of my clients, I see the 10th House as the father and the 4th as the mother - but there are always exceptions.

Psychologically, I look at the impact their upbringing has had on the native and prefer to use the Sun and the Moon as parental indicators. We can lose so much if we stick rigidly to either sex parent in the House placements. I prefer to view the 4th House as the native's early life, our very important psychological foundation.

While the 10th House or Midheaven is achievement, what we stretch up and reach out for, the 4th House is what we stand on, our foundations. What and who we are is rooted in our childhood, the first 7 years. The psychological basis of our unconscious urges and instincts are there in the 4th House. Without strong foundations, we struggle to accomplish anything, or fail to believe that we can succeed in life.

This House represents our emotional, physical and spiritual / psychological foundations. How we were nurtured and our ability to nurture our own children in turn. This is all seen in the 4th House.

We are the slaves to our past but the masters of our future - here lies the axis of the 4th (past) and 10th (future) Houses. Our problems in life often stem from our past (childhood or even our past life) and can only be healed by going back there. Healing begins when we take an objective look at what happened and what beliefs were created.

Our physical home lies here, too. We can see it if we look at the Sign on the Cusp and any Planets inside the 4th House. This House can tell us if we are restless and need to change our home or furniture regularly; whether we love our 'castle' or if we have no place we want to call our own, gypsy style.

It shows our instinctive reactions to life (the instincts and urges of psychology), our past lives and where we are coming from in general.

Interestingly, some astrologers believe that it also represents old age, what we will be like when we get old. It shows the importance of our family, whether we need them or if we can do without - and all the shades in between.

Another way I like to explain the 4th House is to think of it as our psychological foundations that allow us to reach up and grasp the goals and ambitions of our 10th House. If our base is strong, we felt fully supported as children, we will have no trouble reaching upwards. If we felt unsupported throughout our childhood, then jumping up to reach for our goals becomes wrought with difficulties, if not impossible.

I imagine the 4th House as if I was standing on the top rung of a rock solid ladder. If it feels very secure, I can reach just about anything. If that ladder is feeble, unsupported and on unsafe ground, I will not feel safe going farther than the lower rungs. Insecure foundations mean that I hardly feel supported to reach anything in life.

A safe, secure and nurtured childhood leads to trusting that you are able to achieve anything. I don't mean the grand delusions of the psychotic, that is a different matter entirely. I see someone every day whose choices in life have been limited by an insecure childhood.

In practice, I see, on a regular basis, how a solid upbringing leads laying down important psychological foundations. I spend a lot of time taking people into their past to undo the damage done by uncaring or ignorant parents, other adults or children, school bullies and disturbed individuals. This is an important House for the therapist, there are significant clues here as to where the clients' unresolved issues began.

Archetypal Meditation - 4th House

My Meditation: *I have Aries on my 4th House Cusp, this time, he is a crab, complete with a red shell. He laughs as he explains how vigorously he defends my family and home, he is the guardian of this House and takes his role very seriously. He tells me that he had little control over my childhood and schooling, those were circumstances I just had to live through.*

He is now a hermit crab. He shows me that his home is on his back and he takes it everywhere he goes, just the way I take my past with me. It is not about leaving things in compartments, he says, but we are definitely the slave to our past. I have lived most of my life at the teenage hermit crab stage, with a leathery shell. It was not quite hard enough to protect me from hardship. When we toughen up we can manage any challenge much more efficiently, but I was so sensitive that he never really had a chance to harden my shell enough.

He explains that my early sensitivity are his friends, Pisces and Neptune, next door. That plus all those Planets in my 8th House, Chiron on my Ascendant and Sagittarius on my 12th House Cusp. This is why it has been so hard for me to cope with some aspects of life, I have so many powerfully placed psychological Planets. I was thin-skinned, so sensitive, always preparing for crisis, because that's what my experience of life had been so far. This is also what made me what I am today and why I became a psychologist.

Then he closes up, just like a hermit crab does. I take this as an opportunity to merge with him. It feels nice, really safe and secure here, curled up inside my own home, a tough shell protecting me. He has quite a hard carapace now.

I recall how, as a teenager on a camping trip, I spent two nights sleeping inside a small cave. It was awesome, it was like being in the womb, so safe and secure. This is how I feel now. I fall asleep inside that cave again.

Chart Interpretations

Barack Obama - has Taurus on his 4th Cusp with the Moon in Gemini. This shows that he loves his home, his castle. He also thoroughly enjoys just sitting outside on a chair with a cup of home-brewed coffee and a piece of cake - and an encyclopedia. He feels most secure when his family is safe and cozy, comfort is a key word for his 4th House. Barack would probably like to stay at home rather than go to work but there are other factors in his chart that drive him forward. Taurus indicates solid foundations for his ability to step up and achieve his goals.

Hilary Clinton - has Pisces on her 4th House Cusp with the Moon within, it would suit someone who likes to daydream in the safety of their home. Pisces on the 4th Cusp suggests a person who may never have had a home as such, perhaps she never felt comfortable there or she had an imaginary home. It might have been a place of religion, politics, morals and ethics. This is an emotional Water Sign and placing it on the Cusp of the House of childhood also implies that she may have experienced feelings of isolation during her upbringing. It could have been swinging both ways, sometimes bliss and sometimes loneliness. This is hard to determine and we would have to look closely at other factors in the chart.

Justin Bieber - interestingly, Justin also has Pisces on his 4th House Cusp, it contains Venus, the Planet of love, friendships and affection. It suggests that he seeks love and intimacy in his home and family; perhaps his childhood was a mixture of love and loneliness as well. The Venus in the 4th House indicates that he enjoys being at home, that this is where he finds love.

Taylor Swift Facebook Time - Taurus sits on Taylor's 4th House Cusp, suggesting that her childhood was solid, hard working, fun and joy, lots of food and happiness.

Taylor Swift Twitter Time - Scorpio sits on her 4th House Cusp, there are two Planets in her 4th House: Pluto and Mars. These two Planets are both rulers of Scorpio, albeit Pluto is the more dominant of the two. This suggests that there may be problems at home, perhaps abandonment, sadness, or it may be that she just feels that her home or upbringing hold issues she prefers to avoid. The other side of these Planets and Scorpio is transformation and drive, she might be driven to succeed because of opportunities in her childhood.

4th House Planetary Ruler	Moon
Sign Correspondence	Cancer
Angles/Qualities	Angular
Elements / Trinities	Water / Psychological
Health	The stomach and breasts
Keywords	psychological past, upbringing, child-hood to about 7 years, parent, family, House and home, inherited traits, genetic past, conditioning

The Fifth House
friends, interests, hobbies and creativity

This House represents your individuality and your interest in expressing yourself through hobbies, sports, friendships and other activities. It shows your sense of adventure, the books and movies you love, the kind of friends you are attracted to and the activities you enjoy. Here we can see how you like to be entertained, the sports you do and your level of commitment to all of the above. We also find here your talents and interests in music and art - your creativity.

It is also known as the House of casual sex, the people the native is attracted to, whether and how they flirt; the type of casual acquaintances they enjoy. Taurus on the Cusp would seek quiet, determined types, while Sagittarius would want to be with the life of the party. It can also indicate an interest or an attitude to recreational drugs and alcohol.

This is also the House of children as they, too, are the products of our creativity. You can see the native's commitment to their children and how they raise them. It also shows whether they enjoy having kids around or they prefer to avoid them.

It is also the House of gambling and addictions, how the native spends their money in terms of interests, hobbies and the pursuit of happiness.

The 5th House corresponds to Leo and the Sun is its ruler. This suggests that it is the House of sunshine and happiness, as well. It is the home of optimism and by extension a positive outlook on life. It can indicate how you view or deal with buoyant, happy people around you and what you like to do for enjoyment. It is also the people who are drawn to you or whom you are drawn to and how you engage with others to experience joy and happiness. If you are sporty and social, for example, it will be seen in the Cusp Sign and any Planets inside.

If you have an emphasis on this House, a stellium of three or more Planets, it shows that you focus mostly on pleasurable and creative pursuits, sometimes to the detriment of other life experiences. In this case you could become a party animal, take up addictive habits such as alcohol, drugs, gambling or one-night stands, always in search of the next hit.

As a psychologist, I see how this House has the potential to really derange my client's life. Guess who suffers though? Not my client, they are completely oblivious to the damage they are doing to themselves and others. Those hurt the most are their family and loved ones. These people can be overpowered by this House, they can become selfish and self-centered, narcissistic and controlling. It is all about them, their needs and they keep on saying, *"Nobody understands me"*.

Interestingly, these people rarely seek counseling, it is only their parents, their spouses and their children whom I meet instead. Why? Because these natives don't think anything is wrong with them.

I once counseled a young man who was the typical 5th House focused gambler. He even paid me in one dollar coins he had won from his previous night's gambling. He told me that he had come to an end, he couldn't stop his life from falling apart. He simply had no control over his hyperactive and impulsive ways with money, girls, sex, alcohol and drugs. He loved his wife and children, but he was never at home to show it. He ran drug money all over the country to pay his debts, and they were big debts, he was out of control. He told me matter-of-factly that I wouldn't see him again, he was on his last delivery and then they would get rid of him. He was right, I never saw him again.

Archetypal Meditation - 5th House

My Meditation: *this is where Taurus sits, on my 5th House Cusp. I see him as a bull-headed guy, just like the Minotaur in ancient Greek mythology. Interestingly, he helps with my writing and creativity. He is determined, dedicated and prepared to work as long and as hard as needed.*

He is stripped to the waist, he has been chopping wood for the fire. He is outside in a wooded area and has a fire on with a kettle of water just coming to a boil. He hands me a scalding cup of tea, no milk, just how I like it. He turns to me, "What have we got on today, boss?" - "Work, we go to work today, and I need some creativity from you to get through this book I am writing." I reply.

"Yes, I can feel that, it's flowing well today, must be the weather," he says with a matter-of-fact look. I stare out of my office window, it's raining again, and there's a strong, cold wind blowing. It's nice to be inside with nothing else to do but write this book.

I think to myself that Taurus is so simple, he sure looks uncomplicated. He stares at me then extends his hands, palms up. I take them in mine. I sink backwards into my chair and find myself in ancient Egypt and the pyramids, "I built these," he says with such simplicity that I can't imagine anyone else doing it.

I feel awareness flowing from slave to supervisor, then to master and to the pyramids themselves. "I know Taurus, I know," I reply as I realise that he doesn't mean he carved and lifted every block of stone. His contribution was the Taurean template of solid dedication, discipline, determination and creativity that built the pyramids.

He reminds me of my shoulders, he has magnificent woodcutter's shoulders. Mine are sore and aching. "That's what you get for not sticking to a proper typing posture," he says. "I know," I reply, "and if I was chopping wood all day I would have magnificent shoulders too, but I am stuck typing and sitting in a chair all day."

He smiles an old smile, a wise smile, an understanding one, he knows. I decide to stir him a little, "What are you going to do for me today, Mr Taurus?" He blinks, slowly, "Fix your car." Shoot! I'd forgotten. My left headlight is out and I'll be driving home late tonight, in the dark. "I must fix that headlight!" I say to myself.

Sage-like Taurus picks up his ax and goes back to chopping wood. I take that as a sign our meditation is over.

Postscript: I did go outside and look at the headlight, it didn't work, even though I wiggled the wires, pulled it out and pushed it back in three times. I made sure I drove home before it got dark that night. Solid, reliable Taurus, always practical, always the simple path is the best, I like that funny bull-headed archetype.

Chart Interpretations:

Barack Obama - has Gemini on the 5th Cusp showing his interests are broad, he wants to know all. He is concerned about everything to do with humanity. There is no particular focus, anything to do with human interest, society or social justice would appeal to him. He would also attract a lot of people and have lots of friends, he is very social and enjoys social gatherings.

Hilary Clinton - has Aries on her 5th House Cusp, this suggests a very active and passionate sports life, lots of friends particularly involved with physical activity. It can also imply that Hilary is an active seeker of friends and socialises frequently, probably a party goer if that is where she meets them. **Justin Bieber** - Aries sits on the Cusp of his 5th House of friends and fun, he seeks a lot of physical activity to enjoy himself. As a teenager, he would have ample opportunity to indulge in such pleasures. This is the Sign of energy, rushing about, like an 11-year-old boy full of life, hyperactivity even - place that on the Cusp of the House of fun and you can imagine what you get.

Taylor Swift Facebook Time - Taurus sits on Taylor's 5th House Cusp, suggesting that she prefers solid, comfortable activities, fun that involves food and eating, music and pleasures of the physical body. Taurus-type sports include rugby and football.

Taylor Swift Twitter Time - Sagittarius sits on her 5th House Cusp in this chart and the 5th House is loaded with Planets. A stellium of Sun, Uranus, Mercury, Neptune and Saturn, it's busy in here. The House of fun and friendships shows that she is big on friendships and having fun, but she would also like to share it with others. She may be interested in sports in some way, not necessarily practicing herself. The loaded House also suggests that too much emphasis here and she may actually become averse to these activities and seek out solitude and peaceful relationships.

5th House Planetary Ruler	Sun
Sign Correspondence	Leo
Angles/Qualities	Succedent
Elements / Trinities	Fire / Life
Health	The back and the heart
Keywords	individuality, creativity, speculation, friendships, interests, talents and children

The Sixth House
health, work and service

The House of health shows the native's predisposition to physical health, their ability to withstand illness, their inherited weaknesses and what they are susceptible to. By looking at the Sign on the Cusp, it is possible to gain an idea of what the native can expect in terms of health and what advice you can give to strengthen their constitution.

This is a good place to start with if you are involved with natural therapies as it can indicate possible weaknesses in the physical makeup of your patient.

It is also the House of determination and responsibility, how well the native is able to live up to their responsibilities. This can be seen in terms of their commitment to work and level of perseverance. For example, Gemini on the Cusp may be unreliable, or alternatively, they may be driven to work two or more jobs. Taurus may become a workaholic and take on too much responsibility.

This House corresponds to the Sign of Virgo, the Sign of service. Whatever appears on the Cusp is a measure of the native's responsibility to health, work and serving others.

As it also shows the native's work habits, it indicates their ability to work with others, what their supervisor is like, how well they get along with workmates and their boss. It also shows what they are like as managers, as heads of organisations, and how they treat their subordinates. It shows their attitude to work and their employees and their ability to co-operate in a group.

It is also said to be the House of pets, small ones if Gemini is on the Cusp, big ones for Sagittarians and aquatic ones for Pisces. This is an interesting House and raises a lot of discussion when it comes to pets. This is because the House Cusp is only part of the person and can't be taken out of the context of the whole chart. For instance, Sagittarius on the 6th Cusp could hate animals even though Sagittarius is at the top of the list of animal lovers - the native could have other factors in their chart that limits their attraction to animals.

Psychologically, this is the House of service, it acts much like Virgo, serving others. We see how they do this if we look at the Sign on the Cusp and the Planets within. Helping others is sometimes a one-way street, the helper may end up receiving nothing in return.

I see these people in my clinic a lot: they are worn out, often quite resentful. They have no idea how to get out of their situation. They were born to serve, to please others, they never learned about boundaries, limits, or balance.

People with a dominant 6th House can be so sensitive that they get pulled into relationships where they do all the giving. They don't do it to keep the peace, as a Libran does; they do it because they care. It is extremely difficult for these people to learn when to stop. I ask my psychotherapy client to imagine that they are leaning forward so far that they fall flat on their face, completely off-balance. Imagery and metaphor are great teaching aids in my work.

Natives with a dominance or focus on this House, a stellium of three or more Planets, tend to serve all their lives until there is nothing left to give. When they feel empowered to stand up for themselves, their family, partners and children will initially resist and apply pressure to force them to continue as before. Or they might walk out and abandon their beloved giver. There is always resistance when we change. The 6th House native needs to learn how to nurture themselves through this very difficult period of adjustment and abandonment. That's when psychotherapy comes in very handy.

Archetypal Meditation - 6th House

My Meditation: *I have Gemini on my 6th House Cusp, I have worked a little with him in the past so it will be interesting to see what will come up this time. Look at this! There are two of them, chitter chatter, they just can't stop talking. It's Romulus and Remus, the two boys who are said to have founded the Roman Empire.*

"No we didn't," says one. The other twin replies immediately, "Yes we did, but not the way they say." I have no idea who is who or what they are taking about.

"What's that got to do with my 6th House?" I ask.

"We were just commenting on your thoughts about us, that's all." They look at each other and laugh.

They then become adults, dressed in Roman warrior attire, both Centurians. They invite me to sit down at their campfire. Rough and hardened warriors walk and cuss around us. It is cold, the fire smoke swamps down upon us, there is no breeze. The smells of camp life hang in the air.

"We are at the endgame in our struggle to bring things back to balance. Our spies inform us that there are certain weaknesses that we can exploit to pull it off." It's one of them speaking, he looks the part of a powerful leader.

"What are we fighting against?" I ask. The two swing their eyes to look at me.

"We know we are yours to command, but really…" the other says. I am confused and stammer…

"Umm, Gemini 6th House Cusp, no Planets, responsibility, health, service…" I am a bit shocked, what am I supposed to know but obviously don't?

"No, no, no, it's the battle of life, nothing singular. From birth, we have worked to keep you inspired, busy, active, healthy. That's why you have always had interesting jobs and many hobbies and interests." The other says, "If we let you sit around doing nothing, you get lazy, really lazy. We blame Leo for that, he makes you act like a lion, lazing in the sun. It's how we help you stay healthy and centered, by focusing your energies on serving." He sits back and pulls a piece of charred meat from the fire and begins to chew.

"OK, I get that bit, but what's near the endgame?" I ask, still confused.

"Life, you are being set up for the end of your life. It's what we are all doing, as you commanded, setting up a structure for the endgame." He looks at his twin to continue because I am clearly puzzled. "No, not death, that's another adventure. It's your busy retirement, you said that you wanted us to create a busy retirement for you. You know all about it, you told us enough times already." He looks at me intensely.

Obviously, I have forgotten the previous meditations when I invited my archetypes for a chat about my retirement. It is close, I know, I have worked hard on it for years now.

"Yes, now I remember, thanks guys, I do appreciate your support. Is there anything I need to do to help?" I ask. The one sitting by the fire stands up, he walks over to me, he smells of sweat, body odour, smoke and charred meat. He smiles, he does that on purpose to remind me how hard my archetypes have been working.

"Not to worry, get that headlight fixed though, it's no use doing all this work if you get yourself killed." Shoot, that's twice, I am going to book it in right now!

Postscript: yes, the headlight is now fixed.

Chart Interpretations:

Barack Obama - has Cancer on his 6th Cusp showing that he particularly nurtures and cares for his staff and pets. His health issues would include the stomach, fluid retention, digestion, food intolerance and allergies. He would just love a work environment that reminds him of home.

Hilary Clinton - Hilary has Taurus on the Cusp of her 6th House of health and responsibility, she may have issues with her neck and shoulders or with eating too much. Taurus on the 6th also suggests that she is a solid worker who loves going to work, takes on the biggest tasks to accomplish, and completes them ahead of schedule. She is probably very reliable, dedicated and responsible, able to accomplish a great amount of work and she perseveres for a long time.

Justin Bieber - has Taurus on his 6th Cusp showing that he can work long, hard hours, as well, and that his capacity for work is huge. It can also suggest that he may have neck and digestion problems from overeating and can develop allergies if he doesn't pay attention. Taurus is a reliable and responsible Sign.

Taylor Swift Facebook Time - has Gemini on her 6th House Cusp. She is probably a tireless though nervy worker, needs extra time out to rest and build up her energy reserves. It can suggest a nervous stomach and sensitivity to her work environment that may lead to digestive problems. She is reliable, but only when she feels up to it.

Taylor Swift Twitter Time - with Capricorn on her 6th House Cusp Taylor could conquer the world with her responsible work ethic, she is totally reliable and dedicated. Health issues could include bone problems, back, hips and shoulders, and the possibility of arthritis in her joints. However, with adequate exercise and good nutrition there is no reason why she should come down with illness.

6th House Planetary Ruler	Mercury (Passive)
Sign Correspondence	Virgo
Angles/Qualities	Cadent
Elements / Trinities	Earth / Wealth
Health	The intestines, the organs of elimination
Keywords	responsibility, physical health, reliability, service, work environment

The Seventh House
marriage, lovers, romance, clients and customers - the Jungian Shadow

This is the House opposite the Ascendant which makes it very important. It represents the people you are attracted to in intimate ways, like your lovers, partners in business and deadly enemies (those you love to hate). The first House shows how you relate to yourself, the seventh shows how you relate to others.

It is also the House where you project the Jungian 'Shadow'. C. G. Jung explains that the Shadow is composed of all those things, personality traits, beliefs, attitudes, values, etc. that you disown - like anger, frustration, love, kindness, nurturing, calmness, short temper, love of animals, etc.

For example, if we don't want to acknowledge our internalized aggression and we don't resolve them, we will experience this in our 7th house, where other people will hold a mirror for us. They will express our aggression, and usually beat us to it. If we disown or ignore our caring and kind nature then we project it upon our partners and others represented by the 7th House. In other words, others will always reflect the feelings and thoughts we don't want to admit, be it aggression or kindness.

The 7th House is not easy to understand unless we look at it as a way to understand ourselves. This is why we form relationships, so that others push our buttons and we are forced to look ourselves in the eye. The more we are distressed in a relationship, the more we need to look inwards and see what has to be acknowledged and resolved within ourselves.

Most people marry someone who fulfills some of their unconscious psychological needs. They may push their partner's buttons until they leave. They refuse to look deep inside themselves and prefer to blame their partner for their own issues and their inability to manage the relationship. Your partner is the mirror to your own psyche, and as Jung would say, your partner is your Shadow.

The Sign on the Cusp shows what type of person you are attracted to, and how others see you as a prospective partner. If you have Aquarius on the Cusp, for example, then you may be attracted to unusual people, and attract others who seek an unusual partner themselves. It shows your close friendships, closer than your 5th House friends: intimate others, your flatmates, business partners, partners in sports events, etc. Your best friend is also seen here, though this is rather shown by a combination of several factors in the chart.

Because of the psychological nature of the 7th House, the people you are attracted to play an important role in teaching you about yourself. Each person you relate to, even if for a single minute, act as a mirror to your unconscious urges and instincts. They all help you grow psychologically and spiritually. Without your 7th House, you would have no way of knowing your 1st, it is your Mirror in so many magical ways.

The 7th House is also your doctor, dentist, lawyer, client, patient, student, anyone you encounter during legal dealings and court actions. It is how you are seen by the public and what you give of yourself in your relationships.

I always consider this House when I work with people, this is the House of their 'others'. It is therefore the House of the native's guides. Each person who comes into your life is a teacher, they show you something about yourself. You would need to be Sherlock Holmes to work out all the lessons you are given, because it is certainly not an easy exercise.

With the help of Jung's archetype, the Shadow, you experience each person and lesson from back to front, upside down and inside out. Each individual, and by extension, every situation you come across, reveals something about yourself. For example, a stellium of three or more Planets in the 7th House indicates that you seek a better understanding of yourself mostly through your close relationships.

Someone with no or few Planets here learn about themselves mostly through other situations and environments. They may explore who they are through long hard years of self-disciplined, daily exercise, or dedication to a hobby, etc. These natives seek lessons that involve a support network of acquaintances. Not everybody needs close relationships to learn their life lessons. However, a person with a loaded 7th House does. They need many close and intense relationships.

If you have some psychological knowledge, then you may have already observed how people can get caught up in fantasy relationships. They become targeted and groomed by a partner-to-be who often lives on the other side of the world, miles away, or can only meet with them for love and will never let them stay overnight.

This is much more common than I would have thought before I started counseling. These clients are stuck in one-way relationships; they create a fantasy of love that isn't really there. What do their partners get out of this? Money can be an obvious goal - just look at internet relationship fraud, sometimes it's about sex, other times it's help around the house, doing the laundry, or mowing the lawn, building somebody's house… the list is as endless as human greed.

What does this say about the victim's Shadow? Or the perpetrator's?

How do we help these people? I think it is almost impossible. Every shred of evidence you produce has no impact at all. They live in a world of denial and blind hope. Sometimes it seems that the only useful therapy is to wait with them, support them until the penny drops, or until they are discarded. This is a very painful counseling situation, it can take years before the truth dawns on them. Fortunately, if your client trusts you, you should be able to help them pick up the pieces and rebuild their life.

Archetypal Meditation - 7th House

My Meditation: Now we get to see some real action. I have Cancer on the Cusp and Uranus is conjunct (next to it) by a fraction of a degree. Inside, I have Jupiter and Venus conjunct, followed by Mars who is sitting right on the 8th House Cusp. Mars thinks he is too good to be in the 7th and has become part of the 8th House club.

I like meditating on my 7th Cusp, Cancer gives me big hugs; she is nice and cuddly and generous with her love. She is also beautiful like my wife. Cancer is not my wife though, she represents the people I draw to me, close friends, clients and customers, students and acquaintances. Right next to her is Uranus and they get on great. They laugh a lot, they both have a terrific sense of humour; Uranus is just crazy.

I close my eyes and relax back into my chair and begin to breathe slowly and deeply. In and out, I feel myself drop into my inner world as I exhale. I see Cancer running towards me like she always does, maybe she has some of Uranus' energy. I get my hug and a kiss from her, but this is not sexual, it is a genuine friendship.

I have some questions for her and Uranus, in fact for my entire 7th House. So I ask Cancer to call everyone over, Jupiter, Uranus and Venus. We stand on the Cusp line inside the chart. It is a bit like a wharf stretching off into the ocean, ending where Cancer sits on the outer wheel of the chart.

It is evening outside, and it is evening inside me. There is a glow as Uranus walks slowly towards us. Uranus is gleaming, red and radiant, he has so much energy, I can feel it from 20 yards away. I warm myself on his aura. He likes that, he obviously has something on his mind.

He walks to me and grabs my hands. He twists them so hard that I have to bend at my knees. He then swings me around and I enter into his body. I am looking through his eyes and see that I am surrounded by a molten lava landscape.

I am stifling hot, he tells me to be quiet, to just feel and experience, not think (that has become a common theme with my archetypes, they all want me to be quiet and feel, not to think or ask questions). He wants me to feel his heat, his power, to let go and experience this as fully as possible. I am facing forward, standing on the floor of a volcano. There is molten lava below me and in front of me, it sure is hot, sweat is streaming off my face.

I watch as a metal Horoscope melts in front of me, like Salvador Dali's clock, the molten metal is dripping onto the lava floor. Uranus tells me again to be quiet and concentrate. "This is not about astrology," he says, "it's about letting go of astrology and focusing on what I am trying to teach you."

I recall that about a month ago I was writing down a meditation I did with the Tarot Magician archetype. He drove his scepter into the ground beneath my House and charged it with energy. He said that he did it for me and that it would last for about a week. Well it sure did something. The day after, I had a blast of inspiration and started writing this series of psychological astrology books. Here I am a month later and I have almost finished the first book. You can read more about meditating with the tarot archetypes in my tarot course.

I stand inside my chart again, on the wharf - the other archetypes had come to stand next to me. I am still inside Uranus' body, feeling hot and excited, I have heaps of energy. To my surprise, I notice the Magician next to me. I never meditate on both astrology and tarot archetypes at once, what's going on here?

Then Uranus steps out of my/his body and stands next to the

Magician. They then walk through each other. "We share the same mystical space," says the Magician. Uranus nods his head in agreement.

"I wanted to show you that you can cross over from one meditation to the other, a hybrid of archetypes. We all have similar properties, strengths, weaknesses, personalities: tarot and astrology. I am afraid that you have been limiting yourself." Uranus smiles. That's a bit embarrassing, I tell my clients not to limit themselves, and then what am I doing?

"There is enormous power in this 7th House, Noel, and for almost 30 years you haven't noticed it. It's time to utilise our power. Bring us all in to your body, feel us enter your volcano, I don't mind." Uranus' smile broadens even more. I can feel them enter my molten body, merging together but still unique and separate.

There's pressure in my stomach, "Too many people inside me," I think to myself. I suddenly burp and out pops a golden bee from my mouth, a perfectly crafted bee. It reminds me of the bees of Minoan and Greek mythology where they were said to be incarnated souls of good and just people. It reminds me of my good friend, Therese[2], she has a bee icon on her blog.

More bees pop out of my mouth, they fly out by the thousands. "These are the souls you can touch through your 7th House. Kind people, many kind people are waiting to learn from you."

I begin to expand and feel the energies of the archetypes, it is hard though. "Calm down, stop thinking, relax and focus." I ease off too much, it's just so pleasant, I fall asleep.

Postscript: I have tried this several times now and I really enjoy it. So it took me almost 30 years to learn this meditation? It shows that an old dog can learn new tricks.

Chart Interpretations:

Barack Obama - has Leo on this Cusp and this certainly reflects his happy and bright partner, Michelle. Leo on any Cusp generally amplifies the energies of that House in a positive and joyous way. It can also show greed and control, though it's rare. We could say that the people Barack is attracted to are happy, cheerful and generous people, and this is how others perceive him. This is an auspicious and sunny Sign for the 7th House. drawing positive people towards him, who will help him grow spiritually, if he lets them.

Hilary Clinton - has Taurus on both her 6th and 7th House Cusps. This is because the 2nd and 8th - 3rd and 9th Houses are so wide, some Houses have to shrink to fit it all into a 360° wheel. The 6th House is only 21° wide, check: there is 22° on the 7th Cusp minus 1° on the 6th Cusp = 21°. Opposite these two House Cusps are Scorpio on both the 11th and 12th, note that they are the exact same size too. Taurus on this House Cusp suggests that she likes a solid, hard working partner who is reliable and dedicated to his tasks..

Justin Bieber - like Hilary, also has Taurus on his 6th and 7th House Cusps, this suggests that he enjoys being spoiled by his partner, physically. This includes an appetite for sex, as well as cuddles and snuggles. Taurus is physical, he is an Earth Sign, so his partner needs to be physically appealing, a good cook and a good lover, as well.

Taylor Swift Facebook Time - Taylor has the Sign of Cancer on her 7th House Cusp of love and marriage. This implies that she is able to feel and give love. She needs lots of nurturing and she wants to belong, she is very attached to her partner. Love is about hugging and snuggling, as well as feeling loved and appreciated.

Taylor Swift Twitter Time - this chart has Aquarius on her 7th House Cusp suggesting that she is interested in unusual and exciting partners. Taylor also enjoys being in love but only if she can be free, freedom to be herself is most important when looking for a life partner. Love and marriage is not necessarily focal points for the Aquarian 7th House unless there are other features, such as the North Node sitting there. The North Node indicates fated or destined relationships. Only those should be with her whom she is most drawn to. She will know her life partner when she feels like they have known each other all their life.

7th House Planetary Ruler	Venus (Active)
Sign Correspondence	Libra
Angles/Qualities	Angular
Elements / Trinities	Air / Psychological
Health	the kidneys, the bladder and the lower back
Keywords	lovers, partners, enemies, marriage, romance, customers, clients, partnerships in business, court actions, legal contracts, projections and shadows

The Eighth House
evolution, transformation and crisis

This is the second Psychological or Psychic House in the horoscope, it shows the native's dealings with other people's money as a speculator or investor (or gambler), they are accountable for the money of others. It is also the deeper psychological House akin to the 4th House, the first of our three Psychic or Psychological Houses. Here, the native begins to understand their Self through the obstacles in their path, these are to strengthen and push them along on their quest to 'Know Thyself'.

The 8th is the House of crisis, it shows where and how the native deals with climaxes of a psychological and spiritual nature. All crises are psychological and can become spiritual when they are absorbed into the person's psyche, their lesson learned. It is also an occult House indicating the level of our psychic and spiritual power.

Most astrologers do not quite grasp what kind of power is described here. It means that the native has innate or hidden abilities (occult, esoteric), but first they must learn how to exercise them responsibly. If they do not master their 8th House, their power, their lessons will be painful and meaningless.

We see in the case of the shaman and in other occult traditions that the initiate is trained rigorously over long years. They learn to strengthen their psyche, their will and personality to withstand the rigors of the astral plains (the deep psyche), a realm that summons them again and again. If they are able to reach old age they often become masters of their art.

It is not safe to dwell in the 8th House of the deep psyche, unless you know how to protect yourself. This is why the Taoist student and the Yogi spend most of their life in training and in service of their master. This helps form their spirit to become stable, psychologically, emotionally and spiritually balanced. Otherwise, they would be broken under the demands of the 8th House.

I see the 8th House as a cave, Pluto's Cave, a place I go to study and practice my spiritual arts. It becomes the doorway to deeper understanding and can lead to the Underworld. Sometimes this is the deep psyche of the 12th House, at other times it is Pluto's Underworld of the dead, the afterlife, where you will find teachers from other dimensions.

If we delve into these Underworlds without suitable training or natural talent, we can easily burn out. People will do this through drugs, alcohol, or doing advanced kundalini meditations without knowing what they are doing. I am talking about serious neurological damage, nerve damage. Neurotoxins caused by the stress in these unnatural pathways can easily damage the delicate nerves of the brain. This manifests as anxiety, dissociation, depression and even chronic fatigue.

The 8th House demands to be taken seriously, it is 'psychic' but it encompasses more than the 'House of the psychic' or perhaps 'the adept and master'. The 8th House person, who has a stellium of three or more Planets here, is someone who seeks to understand whatever they are interested in at its deepest level. They are not into anything superficial, they only go for what is profound and meaningful. Others might find them quite boring, and they themselves have little patience for chit chat.

It must be remembered that (psychically) sensitive people spend a lot of their time in the unconscious world. Many develop anxiety problems, hang-ups and often experience serious difficulties handling personal relationships. When you see a chart with a focus on the 4th, 8th or 12th House, encourage the native to take up meditation, tai chi or yoga or some other form of mental discipline. This is how they can bring out their innate psychic abilities without burning out psychologically. If they are fortunate, they may even find a therapist, psychologist or counselor who can help them develop specific strategies to manage and fully engage their psychic ability.

The 8th House is also the House of kundalini and sexuality. This can manifest as passion and sexual intensity, driven to experience the thrills in life, particularly sexual orgasm. When kundalini rises to orgasm, it explodes in a magic rush of whole body pleasure. This is very serious sex, definitely not casual, there must be commitment, depth and passion. The 5th House sex is casual, without commitment; the 8th House is the opposite. Here, sex is powerful, not necessarily fun at all, it is taken as a serious expression of Self.

The 8th House sexual act can be enhanced by learning specific tantra techniques that bring the person's life force under control for prolonged orgasm and to leave their physical body for out-of-body experiences. Tantra is designed to train the flow of sexual energy. This becomes part of the native's transformation, helps them rise to other levels of existence.

In terms of health, this House shows how the native transforms illness to health. It is the place for the reproduction and regeneration of tissues and cells for healing. Chi or prana is developed over many years of hard disciplined training, and the masters demonstrate how chi helps the sick to heal. This is similar to Reiki and other forms of hands-on healing. As such, it also represents death and rebirth, transformation and evolution of the spirit or soul.

Healers may learn to use this same energy by going into the Cave of the 8th House and meditate. This House can also encourage astral travel and out-of-body experiences. I started to astral travel soon after I began to practice tai chi, taoist meditation and specific tantra techniques. For nearly 20 years, I left my body almost every night to explore the astral plains. I put this ability down to my 8th House stellium.

Archetypal Meditation - 8th House

My Meditation: *I have Leo on my 8th House Cusp, Mars sits on the Cusp with Leo and the Sun and Pluto are only a few degrees away. They get on great, "Who needs more friends when you have these guys!" They say with a smile and laugh!*

Mercury and Moon sit in the middle of the House, gossiping with each other. They don't care about the boys laughing and singing over by the Cusp. "Like a pack of old men," shouts youthful Mercury. He smiles and so does the Moon, they love their 8th House companions.

I am probably somewhere on the steppes of Mongolia. But I see red sand, it looks more like the Central Australian desert, it's certainly desert country. I see a shaman approaching, he has draped an animal skin over his shoulders, he walks like a tiger, sleek and lean. He is dark skinned, he looks aboriginal.

With a wave of his hand, he beckons me to follow. Then he lifts into the air like a bird of prey. Is it cold up there? I wonder. 'I can do this,' I say to myself and run to leap upwards to follow him.

I am an eagle with enormous wings, I feel myself glide higher and higher. I barely have to flap my wings to stay so high. I feel warm, my body is covered in soft downy feathers. I am now up in the heavens above the Earth itself. It is so exhilarating up here. It soon begins to darken; night is on its way.

I see a fire way below me, the glow touches several faces, one is the shaman's. I alight beside the fire and sit with Leo, Sun and Mars. The Moon and Mercury are opposite and looking into the fire, lost in thought, or perhaps concentrating on something.

The shaman approaches and begins to sing. There is no sound but I feel the vibrations in my chest, I am the song, I tingle like a tuning fork. It centres around my Navel Chakra, the dan tien of taoist tantra. The dan tien begins to expand with energy.

I notice that the man is playing a didgeridoo, he's a powerful aboriginal shaman. As he plays, I am overwhelmed by the vibrations and fall into a deeper trance. My body is now lying on red sand, the sand of the desert in central Australia. I feel myself lift up, out of my body.

Then, right in front of my eyes, I see a deadly poisonous, king brown snake and a huge goanna[3] locked in a fight to the death.

The skin of the snake is absolutely beautiful, it shines brilliant red-brown in the sun… sun? It was night a moment ago. The goanna fights fiercely as it tries to get a better grip on the snake time and again. The snake turns and strikes at the goanna over and over.

I realise that the goanna must be immune to the snake's venom. They twist and turn, each trying to gain the advantage. I am mesmerized, I feel sorry for the goanna because it looks like the snake will win.

The snake is in the pitbull-like jaws of the goanna, pressed firmly into the soft sand. The goanna might be able to swallow a part of the snake, but then the king brown twists away and strikes again and again. Surely, the snake venom will eventually take effect on the goanna lizard, but no, the goanna is as strong as he was at the start. The snake twists and wraps his long body around the goanna, I think it is truly finished this time.

"Enter the snake, feel his power," says a voice in my head. I first put my mind into the snake and then my body, as well, it's easier than I would expect. I can sense his power, it is made of coils and spirals, like tightly wound springs. He twists, turns and then flings his energy into each move. As he relaxes, he draws his strength back into his muscles and ligaments. He won't run out of energy too fast

this way. His muscles and ligaments are where he stores his vigor.

I hear a voice inside my head and I enter the lizard, the Australian goanna. It is quite different from the snake. The goanna's energy appears to be stored in his fat cells, his size and weight are his power. If he can hold his prey long enough, he will use his superior strength and weight to exhaust it. They are both cold blooded reptiles, but each one is very different.

"You have performed the initiation of Snake and Goanna dreaming, a small taste of what is to come if you follow this path. This is a very sacred practice of the original inhabitants of this ancient land, only the shaman and the fully initiated warriors are allowed to learn this dreaming. Respect this practice as you do everything else," says the voice in my head. "When you feel tired use the Sun's energy, like the snake and the goanna, imagine it pouring into your fat cells and into your muscles and ligaments, feel as a snake, or a goanna. This is somewhat different to tai chi which uses bone marrow to store energy. This snake and goanna dreaming method is a quick source of chi. It is fast energy, not the slow energy of the bone marrow chi. Use it to compliment your tai chi exercises."

The voice goes on, "Did you notice the interplay of energy and forms?" I shake my head, I am curious. "They are doing kung fu. Each is perfectly balanced against the other, neither will win. Eventually they will both tire, disconnect and recuperate. Maybe some other time one will win over the other, but not today. This was for you, thank them, please."

I say out loud, "Thank you, snake and goanna, for demonstrating the Tao and sacred dreaming to me today." The snake and goanna stop fighting, they let go. Eyeballing each other suspiciously, they disappear from sight.

I am with Leo, Sun and Mars again, opposite the campfire are Mercury and Moon, sitting beside the fire is the shaman. He is playing the didgeridoo again. I feel a rise of energy from my Base Chakra, it burns upwards along my spinal cord. My head turns into a ball of light but I am in pain, the energy rising to my head feels like it will explode.

I notice that Leo has now taken command, he says, "Calm down, its OK, allow us to be one with you, we will become your 8th House within you. You have done it many times before, but not quite like this. It's alright, relax."

I couldn't do it though, it was too much, the meditation had been going on too long, my head was burning. I quit the meditation. I was exhausted, I went and lay down on my bed and had a power nap. I drew in the sun's energy and charged up my aura like a snake on a rock in the sun. I fell asleep. When I woke up I was quite refreshed and the headache was gone. I will finish this meditation at another time.

This is what an 8th House meditation can teach you. For me it is always about life force (chi), how to move it, circulate it and what to do with it. However, I don't recommend this to anyone without a qualified teacher or inner guide.

At nearly 2 meters in size, this goanna rules his domain on the NSW south coast, Australia.

Chart Interpretations:

Barack Obama - has Virgo on his 8th House Cusp, this suggests that he takes sexual relations very seriously and cleanliness is paramount. We could say that Barack is in charge of other people's money and he takes his responsibilities very seriously. In terms of psychic ability, the Sign of Virgo is not at all psychic, rather, he desires to serve others who have psychic ability. The Sign of service shows he is compassionate, and very passionate about being humane. He may also be quite balanced psychologically.

Hilary Clinton - has Gemini on her 8th House Cusp which indicates that she doesn't fuss too much about her sexuality, it's not something she takes too seriously, she prefers fantasy to actual sexual engagement. Uranus in the 8th House and the Gemini Cusp suggest that she does have some interest in the occult but it's more a passing fancy rather than a lifetime passion. Money and other people's money is interesting, fun and an intellectual challenge that will hold her attention for a while, but it is not a serious activity that she would stick to.

Justin Bieber - has Cancer sitting on his 8th House Cusp, he is probably very comfortable with sexual activities, in fact comfort is the operative word here. Cancer loves the nurturing side of sex, the part where you get together and hug and feel the softness between you. Cancer on the 8th House Cusp will not tolerate infidelity or parallel relationships. This is serious sex and something that must be cherished and nurtured. He will be careful with money but only insofar as it allows him to live comfortably. He will nurture his money, and if given the opportunity, he would be a good accountant.

Taylor Swift Facebook Time - has Leo sitting on her 8th House Cusp, this shows that sex is both serious and fun. It is something she can indulge in big ways, the more extravagant, the more interesting and even more fun. Someone will take care of it for her, as long as she has what she needs today, she will not be bothered about what tomorrow brings.

Taylor Swift Twitter Time - in this chart we see that Taylor has Pisces on the Cusp of her 8th House. This too is committed sexual activity, but it's mostly the pleasure of others. In other words, Taylor would need to watch out that she doesn't get abused by others. The 8th House is also about boundaries, this suggests that she needs to set limits to protect herself from other people's sexual demands. In terms of money, with the weak boundaries of Pisces, it wouldn't be a good idea to ask her to look after your investments. Not that she is untrustworthy, not at all, but she is quite confused and easily led astray and taken advantage of.

8th House Planetary Ruler	Pluto
Sign Correspondence	Scorpio
Angles/Qualities	Succedent
Elements / Trinities	Water / Psychological
Health	the sex organs
Keywords	passion, intensity, serious sex, transformation, crisis, other people's money, psyche, occult, destructive tendencies, power, interest in death, the quest for self-knowledge to help balance emotional and psychic disharmony

The Ninth House
philosophy, higher learning, travel, morals, law and religion

The shift from the 8th to the 9th House shows what we need to handle the stresses of 8th House crises and transformations. The native seeks more education, a solid grounding in philosophy, and they travel all over the world to discover more about their spiritual interests. The 9th House shows the native's tendency to study into adulthood and beyond, to take up tertiary or university courses and to travel to broaden their knowledge of the world.

The 9th House provides life-long education to build the foundations of understanding ourselves through the teachings of others. We need mentors to help us 'see' ourselves, this is why we study and travel to gain that knowledge.

After we have become educated, we seek out professions that will help us practice and refine our skills. This can be in law, morality and religion, philosophy, astrology, psychology. Anything that stimulates the mind and illuminates our path and that of humanity. Eventually, this may become an eternal spiritual quest. At times, it is much like the Quest for the Holy Grail of King Arthur.

Ultimately, the 9th House is our pursuit of spiritual enlightenment. Fortunately other Houses will help us understand whatever we may uncover on our quest. Generally, the 9th House is a place of higher learning, and together with other indicators in the chart, we use it to form an image of the native's spirituality.

This is also the House of education, it shows how knowledgeable the native wishes to be, especially in terms of common sense and whether they want to continue their studies. We travel to gain insight and wisdom, thus this is the House of long-distance and world travel.

Here we gain wisdom and experience life by visiting far away places.

By looking at the Sign on the Cusp and any Planets within the 9th House, we fathom the native's aptitude for higher learning, morality and wisdom, or the lack thereof.

A focus on this House by a stellium of three or more Planets suggests that the person has also taken on some of the qualities of the corresponding Sign, Sagittarius and its Ruler, Jupiter. Their Mutable Fire energy is easily ignited and they want to engage in the adventure of the chase. They often party all night long. They may resort to mind-altering drugs and other exciting and unorthodox methods on their spiritual quest. This might include religious practices such as whipping, self-flagellation, dancing, abstinence, fasting, pilgrimages or the contemplation on religious texts.

An interesting point to note is that Sagittarius is generally accepted as the Sign of the centaur with the lower body of a horse and the upper body of a human. Some versions of the ancient Greek myth of Sagittarius, however, mention Crotus, a satyr who lived on Mount Helicon in Greece.

Some satyr illustrations look like the Greek god, Pan. Satyrs look human except their two hind legs, which resemble a goat or a horse. Some also have the horns of a goat or the ears of a horse. Like Chiron, Crotus was a musician, noted for his wisdom and he was a hunter, too. He is said to have invented the bow and arrow.

If we consider the centaur side of Sagittarius, then we see that they were wild and rowdy creatures given to drinking, sex, fighting and debauchery. Sometimes a focus on the 9th House leads the native towards the animal form of the untamed, drunken centaur. When we consider the satyr side, we see an entirely different personality. This is the serenity of the wise Crotus, he demonstrates the elevated qualities of Sagittarius.

Psychologically, this is the House of wisdom and morality, as well as the narcissistic party animal and the criminal. Our prisons are filled with centaurs.

I rarely see a true, centaur-type Sagittarian for counseling, mostly because they know better. They believe that they are smarter than their therapist, they know more about psychology and counseling, they are very savvy. They enjoy playing mind games during the session to get the better of the professional they are facing.

This is particularly so in the case of the narcissists who are dragged to counseling by their irate partners. They don't want to be there; in their mind they don't need therapy. Besides, if they wanted counseling, they would do it themselves. I rarely see these extremely narcissistic, centaur Sagittarians, but I do see a lot of their partners.

These centaur Sagittarians remind me of the story about the donkey who found a pile of books and wanted to prove to everyone that he really was a smart donkey. Donkey had always been called stupid, "stupid donkey!" everyone would shout at him. It really hurt his feelings. So when he found a pile of books he stacked them carefully on his back and proudly paraded back and forth in front of the other animals.

All the animals were extremely impressed by how bright the donkey was. They talked among themselves, "Donkey must be so smart." But in the back row, there was a wise lion who cried out, "You may have a pile of books on your back but you are still a stupid donkey!" The animals turned around and gawked in horror. The donkey himself swaggered towards the lion pushing through the crowd of admirers. "Don't you see how smart I am, Lion, I have a library of very serious books on my back, I must be smart."

The lion stood up, towering over the donkey, "Donkey, unless you have read every one of those books and understood each line, you will remain just a stupid donkey with a pile of books on your back." And with those words of wisdom, the lion walked away.

A few centaur Sagittarian or 9th House dominant people are just like the donkey, they think they know everything.

Some natives with a focus on the 9th House end up in jail. That may be because they have no morals, with so much focus on the 9th House, their morals become self-serving. They are often narcissistic to the point of being delusional. Ask any of the centaurs sitting in jail if they were guilty of their crime, none will admit it; it is always someone else's fault.

This is an important facet of an overly dominant Fire Sign, in particular Sagittarius and Jupiter. One path leads to gentle and wise Crotus, the other path to the wild, wilful and wicked centaurs. There are plenty of resources available on narcissists and psychopaths; they will also be discussed in more detail in my courses and prospective books.

Archetypal Meditation - 9th House

My Meditation: *I have Virgo, the Sign of service and caring on my 9th House Cusp, no Planets reside there. When I close my eyes and enter my 9th House, I see Virgo standing alone. She is stunning in her thin Virgin's gown, she looks classical ancient Greek. I tell her so and she smiles as she walks towards me, we embrace. I can feel such a force of love, it pierces my heart and I become overwhelmed. I fall on the floor of the temple. Next, I find myself in a modern bed, Virgo singing a song of my childhood, a nursery rhyme.*

I look around and I notice that I am in my childhood home. I am about 5 or 6 years old. I get up from my bed and notice that I am wearing Y-fronts (to my sister's eternal horror, but I hated pj's). That is embarrassing so I quickly grab some shorts and put them on. The linoleum on the floor is cold, but I don't care. I walk out of my room and into our family kitchen.

My father is up and having breakfast, it is not quite dawn. My mother is cooking his breakfast and she places a bowl on the table in front of me.

This is a memory of our early morning ritual, Mum, Dad and me. Of my three siblings, only I enjoyed getting up so early. I loved mornings, I would get up before everyone else and rejoice in the day. I was alone and it was all mine. I keep on doing that to this day. I used to feel like a king being the only one up, except on my Dad's workdays of course.

My mother would get up every morning no matter what time my father had to start work, be it summer or winter, rain, hail or shine. My mother was a servant in our house, a happy one. Together we would eat our breakfast, not saying much. My father no doubt was preparing his mind for the day ahead. I felt sorry for him, all he did was work and come home very late. I knew that he did it for us. He, too, was a servant to his family. Later on he began to drink and came home in a bad mood.

It was this breakfast scene that reminded me of my own life. At an early age, I decided I didn't want to work the same was as my father.

My mother, a typical mother of the era, was always happy to make something at the drop of a hat - a meal, a drink, a cowboy's suit. Everything was homemade. Service, studying hard, working hard to get ahead, staying out of the rut. Did my dream work for me? Maybe Virgo has the answer, she nods, it's the same answer I have myself.

Chart Interpretations:

Barack Obama - has Scorpio exactly at 0°18' on his 9th House Cusp. I want you to look closely at this, 0 degrees and 18 minutes, just past the very end of Libra at 29°59' (remember, all Signs are all exactly 30° in width). If the Earth spins 1° every 4 minutes, it is just over a minute that separates very early Scorpio from very late Libra on his 9th House Cusp. Interesting isn't it? It's a reminder that an accurate birth time is critical for accurate House Cusps.

Barack's Scorpio Cusp suggests that he is a zealous student of life seeking answers to the questions of law, morality, human interest and perhaps travel. He seeks to understand these topics deeply. He is not satisfied to study at a superficial level, he needs to know the subject thoroughly. We could say that Obama wants to understand himself by figuring out the laws of humanity. With Scorpio on the Cusp, we could safely say that he takes morality very seriously and works towards making the world a more ethical place. Neptune resides in his 9th House suggesting that he sometimes feels at sea when overwhelmed intellectually, he needs strategies to be able to re-focus and come back to Earth if that happens.

Hilary Clinton - Hilary has Cancer on her 9th House Cusp suggesting that she feels nurtured and safe when studying and on the road, these activities are comforting. In this instance, traveling would not be so much fun, but it would make her life more secure and emotionally rewarding. She has three Planets sitting in her 9th House: Mars, Pluto and Saturn, which suggest that she focuses a lot of her time on learning and travel. A deep appreciation of morality, law and ethics helps her feel safe and secure. It is not rules and regulations that limit her but her need for comfort and her sensitivity.

Justin Bieber - we see that Justin has Leo on his 9th House Cusp and Chiron, the 'wounded healer', is sitting inside. This suggests that Justin has strong arguments for and against certain morals and ethics. He would love to discuss this with any audience who would sit long enough to listen. The 'wounded healer' there suggests that at times he has felt immorally or unethically used. Perhaps he has been deeply hurt, wounded, or morally abused by someone. Without doubt, this stimulates his passion to make a stand of his own.

Taylor Swift Facebook Time - Libra sits on Taylor's 9th House Cusp suggesting that she is liable to compromise her own morals for her peace of mind. This is the Sign of balance and harmony, so Taylor would probably rather adjust her own ethics to accommodate others than make waves or bring disharmony into her relationships. Libra is also the Sign of justice, she may have an interest in law, morality, religion or ethics and seek to establish these qualities in her own life. She delights in travel, she might enjoy visiting far away places and bring back plenty of goodies. She is presumably attracted to bright, glistening objects, jewelry and clothing, everything beautiful. This placement can sometimes emphasise the Libran shortcut of compromise.

Taylor Swift Twitter Time - with Aries on her 9th House Cusp we could say that Taylor makes sure that her life and the life of those around her are in line with her principles. This is a very aggressive and strict Sign that would not tolerate any wishy-washy religious or immoral behaviour in others or herself. She would find it difficult to stand by and watch others treated immorally or unethically.

Notice that changing her birth time by about 12 hours has completely changed her personality. That's why an accurate birth time is critical.

9th House Planetary Ruler	Jupiter
Sign Correspondence	Sagittarius
Angles/Qualities	Cadent
Elements / Trinities	Fire / Life
Health	the thighs and liver
Keywords	wisdom, higher learning, long distance travel, philosophy of life, life experiences

The Tenth House

midheaven, Medium Coeli (MC), career, ambition, success, what and how we strive to achieve

This 10th House Cusp shows the direction the native is heading, their purpose and their ambitions. The 10th House and Midheaven are the same except for a shift in emphasis. When we refer to this House as Midheaven, we primarily think of direction, and when we refer to it as the 10th House, we mainly think of ambition and achievement.

As mentioned previously, the Midheaven is what we are reaching up towards. It requires good and strong foundations (4th House) to achieve greatness, otherwise the native needs to draw upon other factors like the 9th House of education, or the 7th House of a supporting partner, or perhaps their 1st House of natural talent and a solid constitution.

The 10th House shows the native's appearance in the public eye and the Sign on its Cusp tells us about how they are seen and how the public feels about them. It also shows the type of career they are driven towards and whether they take on a public or private profile. Whether they are seen by others (e.g. they work behind a shop counter serving people or they present news on national television) or if they work behind the scenes (detectives, historians, researchers, etc.).

As it is at the top of the chart, this House is visible directly above our heads and acts like a beacon or light. Planets aspecting or touching the Midheaven take on greater importance and are often the most powerful Planets in the chart. Look upon the Midheaven as a light shining down upon the rest of the psyche and you will begin to understand its significance and power.

This is also the House of authority and whether the native bows down to authority figures or is a rebel. It indicates how they handle being told what to do by someone in a position of authority. It is leadership potential, what style of leader they may become, and their ability to work with others in a supervisory role.

It can show whether they are able to make their own breaks in life or they need to be pushed and shoved along to get ahead. Self-starters have strong Midheavens as well as other powerful chart factors.

This is also the House of the strong or disciplinary parent. Traditionally, it is the mother but the controversy is not settled. It is best read as the House of the parental figure who helped the native strive to achieve their best. I generally see it as the native's father but this is not a fixed rule.

Psychologically, this is the second Angle I look at when I draw up a chart. The first is the Ascendant and any Planets in the 1st House, followed by the Midheaven and everything in the 10th House. These two are signal Houses, they give me a quick summary of the individual, their strengths and weaknesses and what is driving them. The Sign on the Midheaven shows where and how the native seeks to succeed, to get ahead in life and their drive to survive.

I always look for Planets in the 10th House, as this gives me some clues as to how much they put into their therapy and recovery. Are they driven to succeed in life and therefore in therapy? It is only part of their entire psyche, I know, but the Midheaven and the Ascendant are quick and simple indicators of their personality. Once I have checked these two Cusps and Houses, I move to the Luminaries, then the personal Planets and I slowly work myself deeper into the chart.

The lesson here is to never underestimate how much information we can extract from a single House.

Archetypal Meditation - 10th House

My Meditation: I have Libra on my 10th House Cusp or on the Midheaven (MC). Inside the 10th House sits Neptune next to my MC, and Saturn is in the middle of the House. Libra will compromise and harmonise, while Neptune will blend, dissolve and disguise. Saturn is determination and ambition and he will always push and drive. Does that mean that my 10th House is about striving to achieve Saturnian goals? Or that sometimes I lose my direction in the mists of Neptune, while Libra makes me compromise instead of seizing what I want? Does it mean that my quest for success is doomed?

I close my eyes and relax, breathing slowly in and out as I begin to sink into trance. I then stand in the centre of my natal chart and look towards my 10th House Cusp. I see my archetypes standing and waiting for me, they are quite happy to meet me again.

Neptune is once again a cartoon character, a merman, the God of the Seas. He holds a rod from the tarot deck, but on a second look I think it is just his trident. Libra is enormous. I have never seen her loom so large in my meditations. She towers above the entire chart. Libra, as my Midheaven, wants to demonstrate how important she is.

These Greek Goddesses are always beautiful and Libra is no different. She changes her appearance every second, appearing in the many guises of the Justice card from the tarot deck. She portrays blind justice, too, just like the marble statues outside a court house. Her last change is into the Yin Yang symbol of Taoism, balance and harmony. OK, I understand now.

"I am a filter for your energies, I am responsible for the right balance between your ambition, the drive of Capricorn, your powerful yet wild Leo stellium, the passion and intensity of your 8th House, and, of course, Saturn, the Lord of your Chart. These forces place

enormous pressure on me to filter what is worth chasing and worth allocating my precious resources to. Neptune sits with me as the Planet of High Degree, together we help govern your path, we guide your ambitions." Libra is now back to human size.

Libra continues, "All your life you have sought out silly jousting quests and wasted your energy. You have enormous capabilities but you can go off like a firecracker and waste it all in one explosion of energy." Neptune makes an image, a sparkling wick dowsed with a drop of water from his finger. It sizzles as it goes out.

"We work together, Neptune and I, Saturn is usually too busy with his own work to contribute much, and sometimes he even gets in the way. His energy is too Earthy for us to understand, so we let him do his own thing." I notice that Saturn isn't even listening to her, he appears to be thinking, absorbed in a world of his own.

"You can help us by meditating just as you are doing now. Listen when you work with your clients, listen to what you guide them to do and follow your own advice." Hey but I do, I protest. "No you don't, you become distracted." I hate to admit it but I am a bit lazy, and it isn't nice to have this pointed out in public by my own archetype. "Don't worry, no one will laugh, everyone is lazy in their spiritual pursuits, everyone. I should know, I am an archetype." Libra smiles, I notice her dazzling teeth flash.

As if on cue, Saturn walks over, he has been on his own throughout our conversation. As though taking centre stage in a play, "I just want to add that I am very pleased with your work ethic. You charge ahead and complete each task that Capricorn and I set for you. We are working hard to make your achievements as easy as possible. It's those others over there who constantly check your forward momentum." Saturn points at the 7th and 8th Houses, he *then points at Chiron on the Cusp of my Ascendant. "They seem to think you can live without a roof over your head, but it's our efforts that provide that roof and the food to feed your family."*

Saturn isn't finished, "We work tirelessly while you sleep to prepare your day ahead, but sometimes your friends, the other archetypes, enjoy putting things in the way to trip you up. It makes extra work for us, and for you." He can be a wet blanket, but I have to admit that he has a good point.

Saturn and Jupiter have been arguing most of my life (they are in a Square aspect), but lately they have been quite good friends. Jupiter walks over, he takes Saturn's outstretched hand and shakes it warmly. "My old friend, things have changed. Our projects to lay spiritual foundations are going well and that in itself aids your tasks, why not ease up a bit? We should all work together."

I get bored, I have been through this with Saturn and Jupiter before. Even though the entire exchange only takes a minute I want to talk more with Libra and Neptune. Especially Neptune, he is a really hard dude to get to know. I notice that Jupiter is now standing with Saturn, they stop talking and turn towards me.

"Neptune, would you please take Libra and myself to your home and teach me to harmonise in your element of Water?" I ask, looking at both he and Libra.

"Of course," gurgles Neptune, I am sure he is holding a tarot rod as we disappear into his mists.

I begin to breath slowly and deeply again. I start to practice the snake and goanna breathing. I imagine that I am lying on a rock soaking up the warmth of the Sun into my muscles and fat cells.

My body is filled with warm water instead of energy and light, it is like sparkling mineral water. I begin to see my life unfold like a movie screening right there in front of me. Episodes of my many failed ambitions pass before my eyes, and I experience each failure again. I feel a pain in my chest as if I wanted to cry at each scene of frustration, humiliation and despondency. So many garden paths, so many missed opportunities, so many wasted years.

Somehow, I become an old sea snail on the sandy floor of a beach, just behind the breaking waves. I am washed gently back and forth with the waves. I am rocking, back and forth; so peaceful and gentle, it is soothing. The ache in my chest begins to ease. I feel the rough emotional edges wearing away as I am softly brushed along the sandy floor.

I remain the size of a snail when Neptune swims over to me and with a welcoming smile signals for me to follow. We dive deeper and deeper towards the dark entrance of an underwater cave, his home, at last. I am quite surprised because there is a huge crowd to greet us, waving, shouting and cheering. It is like Harry Potter walking triumphantly down Hogwarts Dining Hall. I make a bow and leap like a dolphin somersaulting high into the air. I am back to my happy self.

Neptune just showed me a new meditation, lying on the ocean floor, rocking back and forth, it is a simple technique to alleviate my sadness.

Postscript: I have tried this in combination with the 11th House meditation, the waves rolling up my body, then down again. Honestly, it is fantastic and so calming.

Chart Interpretations:

Barack Obama - has Scorpio on his 10th Cusp which tells us that he must be in control. He may strive to succeed ruthlessly, passionately and with great intensity. Success for the Scorpio can be an issue of life and death, so Obama can see his ambitions in terms of life achievements. If he cannot achieve his goals, he has failed in life.

Hilary Clinton - Virgo is on Hilary's 10th House Cusp, she has to gain an understanding of 'service'. Virgo is the Sign of order, caring and neatness, it's also the Sign of cleanliness. I would expect her to be very neat and tidy. Her ambitions are geared towards helping to provide others with what they need, not necessarily what they want. Virgo is a functional and pragmatic Sign, it is about action, not theory or philosophy. She strives to accomplish practical goals.

Justin Bieber - has his Midheaven in Virgo, he too seeks to find an understanding of service to others, perhaps even to the entire human race. All that is required to activate this House is to look at the ruling Planet of Virgo: Mercury. I really don't want to go into the Planets here, but let me share with you an astrological secret. Each House has a Sign on its Cusp, as discussed in this book, and each Sign is ruled by a Planet. In the case of Virgo, it's Mercury.

If you look for Mercury, you will find it in Justin's 3rd House. Mercury then brings its Signs, Gemini and Virgo, into the House it resides in. Thus we have Gemini 'intercepted' or hidden in the 7th House, and Virgo is on the Midheaven or 10th House Cusp. Mercury now gathers the 7th House and the 10th House into his 3rd House. It's like bringing your family together for an occasion. The 3rd House has become very busy with four Planets and two additional Houses. We now read the 3rd House as being related to Justin's 10th House and vice versa. In other words, his mental activity is driven towards the ambitions and achievements of the 10th House, as well as towards his partner or lover.

Taylor Swift Facebook Time - the Sign on the 10th House Cusp, or Midheaven, is Scorpio, and it is ruled by Pluto, sitting right in the middle of the 10th House. This suggests that she may be controlling and ambitious, passionate and intense to achieve what she strives for. Scorpio is driven to control their environment to ensure that they are psychically or emotionally safe. Safety, security and betrayal are big words for a Scorpio, and they really fear abandonment, they would do anything to stay safe. That's why control is so important for them. Anyone who tries to take command while she's working should take cover.

Taylor Swift Twitter Time - her Twitter birth time of 8:46 p.m. means that she has Taurus directly above her. Taurus is much more gentle than Scorpio, that's for sure. All they need is some good food, a bed to lie on, some soft music and a cuddle and they are in heaven. Taurus Midheaven implies that she will work solidly and steadily to achieve her goals. She can be very reliable, steadfast and stubborn to get what she wants. Not that she will demand anything from anyone. No, her resolve is to complete her goals at her own pace, in her own manner. If anyone wants to help that's fine, if they want to take command, that's fine too, as long as they don't stand in her way.

10th House Planetary Ruler	Saturn
Sign Correspondence	Capricorn
Angles/Qualities	Angular
Elements / Trinities	Earth / Wealth
Health	the knees and skeletal structure
Keywords	ambition, achievement, career, public image, authority figures

The Eleventh House

humanity, compassion, empathy, intuition, hopes, dreams and wishes

This is an interesting House, which is not easy to define. It involves our unconscious urges and instincts as they rise to enter our conscious world to manifest change for the good of humanity. This manifests as hopes for ourselves and for others, how we go about realising our dreams of improving humanity and what we wish for others.

The 11th House shows the organisations we join to improve ourselves and make the Planet a better place, like Green Peace, Lions Club, Rotary or Little Athletics.

It is the House of our attitudes towards humanity and the Earth as a living entity, our dreams, fantasies and our contributions to their realisation in our lifetime.

This is a social House and we can see how the native socialises and what sort of people they are attracted to when they want to see the bigger picture. In fact, this House is the bigger picture itself, it is not a personal House. It shows the native's ambitions (or their lack) for the greater benefit of humankind and nature. The person's humanitarian interests are shown here, as well as their ideals for the improvement of the world as a whole.

Psychologically, this House is also difficult to understand. It is an Air House, Succedent and public, it has everything going for it, but I find it problematic. I see a loaded 11th House, with a stellium of three or more Planets, and the person seems to be thoroughly engaged in external activities and organisations.

At first, that was the biggest clue to their personality. Then I went on to discover that they are frequently engaged with humanitarian organisations such as medical charities, social clubs and animal welfare associations. It seems they are driven to help and be part of the committee, but it can also become a form of intellectual distraction. If they get busy enough, they can avoid facing how their own world is falling apart.

A focus on the 11th House is not at all a psychological problem. There is nothing wrong or psychologically damaging in being involved in raising awareness of certain medical treatments, saving the wolves, or any other cause. The problem arises when they have psychological or emotional issues that they refuse to deal with. For example, Saturn conjunct Venus or Moon in the 11th House may represent a doomed relationship that they are avoiding to confront. When they run away from their emotional issues they fail to heal or grow. The 11th House is where some people escape from their emotional reality.

In these situations once they have made the decision to seek support in counseling, they can begin to heal. 11th House people are generally quite intelligent, focused and motivated to help, but their Air traits make them prone to avoid reality. They are often great conversationalists, knowledgeable, charming and keen to learn how to help themselves. They respond well to relaxation, enjoy solving problems and they are happy to discuss what is really going on in their lives.

What works best is to let them talk about their interests, they need to be heard. I do an awful lot of listening and through listening I begin to understand them and we can work out the best therapeutic approach to meet their needs and suit their personality. This way they are validated, *"I felt heard.'* is their most common response. When you are working with an 11th House client, do your best to listen and validate what they say, that's the best thing you can do for them.

Archetypal Meditation - 11th House

My Meditation: *I have Scorpio on my 11th House Cusp and the North Node is inside, I notice a huge scorpion standing on the outer wheel of the chart. I am standing on a beach and it is getting close to evening. I am on the west coast of Australia, the rising Moon is behind me. The scorpion stalks towards me and stings me in the chest, shoot that really hurts! Streams of green liquid spurt out of me onto the wet sand, the pain begins to subside. Then the scorpion speaks to me. He explains that this is the pain I have stored up from working with so many wounded souls.*

"You hold on to their pain too much, I know you try not to and that you have techniques that you practice, but it still gets to you. Some of your clients get inside you, that's not healthy." The scorpion then walks away.

I chase after him, "What should I do?" I ask.

"Tonight I gave you a gift and released your built-up pain, but you need to learn to do this for yourself. Lie down here on the beach, close your eyes and go into trance."

I am lying on the wet sand, it is evening, a dazzling white Moon is rising in the east. I close my eyes and start to breathe slowly and deeply. I center my breathing in my dan tien, the Navel Chakra. The scorpion stands next to me.

"Remember your heart meditations many years ago?" Yes, I certainly do, it nearly killed me. "Yes, I know, you went way too fast. You weren't ready for all that power, but you did it and we are all proud of you for trying."

He is referring to my years of practicing tai chi and taoist meditations that led me to open all seven chakras. It took eleven years of dedicated practice. When I opened my heart chakra for the first time, it exploded, I felt like I had been electrocuted. My whole body shook for a full minute, maybe even longer. I was in a state of bliss for days afterwards.

From that moment on, I could feel pure love at any time, like a switch, overwhelming love, love so powerful it would sometimes knock me unconscious. I opened it so often that it eventually stayed open and that became very painful, very dangerous. I would swing from one emotion to another as I took on the feelings of each person who walked by. I had to close it down and only open it a tiny bit during meditation. I was not strong enough to manage such powerful kundalini energy at the time.

"Yes that's what I am talking about, it's time to work on it again. Slowly, very slowly, we will guide you."

"You've got to be joking."

"Not at all, it's time. We won't let you open too fast, not this time, do this wave meditation, it will be OK."

I am in trance on the beach, I feel the waves flowing up to my chin and then slowly back down to my feet, up and then down. It is moving tension and stress from my heart and out through the feet.

"Earthing, your key to this process is earthing. When excess kundalini sits in your heart it will hurt like before. This exercise trains excess chi to travel down your body and out through your feet, it is a safety measure. You know all this from your tai chi, remember to earth, at work and at home." The scorpion then stands at his outer wheel post just like he did when I arrived.

I continue doing the water earthing exercise for the next few minutes. It is pleasant and calming, then I fall asleep.

Postscript: I could feel the energy in my heart centre but I was terrified to go to the next stage, I wanted to negotiate with the scorpion to wait until I am ready. It was like standing at the edge of a swimming pool knowing full well how painful it would be to jump into the icy water.

Chart Interpretations:

Barack Obama - has Sagittarius on the Cusp of his 11th House, showing that he likes to shoot his arrow into the air and takes great pleasure and joy in finding where it lands. We would say that he is adventurous in his desires for humanity, that he is spirited and holds up exalted moral standards to all people. It suggests that he has high aspirations to help others and the environment, In fact, Sagittarius is itself morality, religion and law, for everyone's benefit.

Hilary Clinton - Libra sits on the Cusp of her 11th House and Neptune is inside. Libra is the Sign of balance, justice and compromise. Her wishes for humanity are justice, peace and harmony, very high aspirations indeed. How will she realise these ideals in such a wild world? On the one hand, she has the support of Neptune, the Planet of Water, which helps her feel the needs of humanity. And on the other hand, there is Libra, an Air Sign that can make plans to solve the problems at the root of this pain. Here we have emotion and intellect working together. At times she will feel that she has let everyone down (Neptune) and she will worry (Libra).

Justin Bieber - has Libra on his 11th House Cusp and he has the Moon inside. Here we see that he has the desire (or urge) to better the Planet by bringing peace and harmony to humanity. His songs certainly do bring a lot of happiness; so he is successful in that respect. This is an interesting placement for the Moon. The Moon is feminine, it is Water, so it is emotional, and it also represents the public, as well as home and family.

His songs connect people, homes, families, individuals and society as a whole. Songs of love are songs of emotion, nurturing and caring. In some ways, Justin is fulfilling his 11th House desires to bring peace and harmony to the world more successfully than most could ever dream of.

Taylor Swift Facebook Time - look at her tiny 10th, 11th and 12th Houses, and then check the corresponding 4th, 5th and 6th Houses. They are the same, they have exactly the same House Cusp degree. Now notice those extra large Houses, the 1st, 7th, 2nd and 8th and see that they are opposite each other. Next, look at her Twitter time 12 hours later, the Houses are much more balanced in size, none of them stand out as very large or very small. We compare the two versions of her chart because we don't have her exact time of birth. This is a great way to learn that accurate birth time is very important.

Taylor has Scorpio on her 11th House Cusp, it shows control, passion and intensity. We already mentioned Scorpio's fear of abandonment and betrayal. They are scared of being left alone, so they control all they can to stay safe. Well, the 11th House is about people's welfare, and it can certainly trigger her own issues. We would expect compassion for others who are abandoned, betrayed and lonely. Maybe this could drive her to build, fund or find shelters or half-way Houses for the poor and marginalized in our society. She would do this with great intensity and passion.

Taylor Swift Twitter Time - has Gemini sitting on her 11th House Cusp for this birth time, it also has Jupiter, Moon and Chiron, a mini-stellium sitting inside. This is a powerful House, and one that shows her approach to healing the Planet and saving souls.

Gemini is our first guide, our first signpost to what Taylor wishes to do and how she does it. The strength of Gemini is communication. If we add these three powerful Planets, we have planetary focus here. Planets in a House show us where the native focuses all that power. The Moon is society and emotion, empathy and nurturing. Jupiter is amplification, generosity and adventure, while Chiron is her wound. If we bring all these together, we come up with a desire and an instinctual urge to help those less fortunate than herself.

11th House Planetary Ruler	Uranus
Sign Correspondence	Aquarius
Angles/Qualities	Succedent
Elements / Trinities	Air / Relationships
Health	the nervous system, the ankles
Keywords	humanitarian, dreams and wishes for the future, friends and associates in clubs and other organisations, ideals and fantasies about helping the Planet

The Twelfth House

dissolving in the deep unconscious

This House is totally subconscious and shows us how the native copes with emotional and psychological stress and whatever the native wishes to suppress from consciousness. This is the abode of those skeletons in the closet that psychotherapy attempts to bring into the open. The native will generally do anything to keep them locked up because they are too frightening, like nightmares. In extreme cases of anxiety, they can push the person over the edge.

It can also be likened to incarceration, imprisonment or institutionalisation, wrongly or otherwise. The 12th House experience is that of being trapped or imprisoned, particularly if the native is not comfortable with the affairs of the House.

One role of astrology is to locate and point out the strengths and shortcomings in the native's personality. The 12th House can indicate the person's weaknesses that compel them to run away from life, but it can also reveal their power which allows them to meet the world and overcome pain and suffering.

Signs on the 12th House Cusp and any Planets within indicate how the native copes with life, how they express themselves from a spiritual perspective, and whether they can communicate their wisdom. It can also show the emotional honesty of the native, whether they run away from responsibility, or they express their innermost self honestly and openly once they have dealt with their 12th House (psychological) issues.

The psychic effect of the 12th House is seen when the native's conscious and subconscious selves are balanced. Without this, the 12th House psychic begins to channel their own subconscious issues and fantasies. When balanced, they are in tune with their higher selves and that of others. Be aware that some clairvoyants or psychics channel their own unresolved 12th House issues and fantasies.

The best way to deal with the 12th House is to meditate or at least learn some discipline that forces you to deal with your innermost fears. Counseling, in the form of psychotherapy, works with the unconscious and is often crucial when dealing with 12th House issues.

Natives with a strong 12th House have powers beyond mere mortals, but they first need to come to terms with this before they can use it constructively. Such a person will often end up in psychological distress if they don't undergo the necessary training. There is nothing pleasurable about experiencing frightening nightmares every night.

This is the House of the deepest unconscious, the third psychological House, and as such, it is dangerous to enter for those untrained. It can be a source of psychological discomfort for most natives who have personal Planets here. These people are best directed to attend counseling, psychotherapy, practice tai chi, yoga or some other grounding meditation. One of the best things these natives can do for themselves is to learn how to earth or ground themselves.

There is a saying, *"The psychotic drowns in the same waters in which the mystic swims with delight."*[4] The mystic or adept can move safely and freely in their inner world. The psychotic or dabbler who has not learned the discipline of living in the unconscious, however, is at risk of drowning. This is especially so if they rely on drugs to open the doors of perception. It tells us a lot about the dangers of experimenting with deep psychological states without adequate training.

If you look at the 4th and 8th Houses, you will see the progression of psychological and spiritual development. They form the three Houses of psyche, spiritual evolution and karma.

Psychologically, this is a Power House. Many people have the 12th House highlighted through a planetary stellium. Its role is to dissolve consciousness and get ready for the next evolutionary phase. This may be why it is so hard to work with Planets here. The meditator has to go so deeply within to find those hidden gems that they are tempted to just dissolve into nothingness.

When someone has a stellium or other emphasis on the 12th House I usually approach them very slowly and gently. They are like everybody else in many ways. They get through life, and they have developed their own ways to manage, like we all have.

Sometimes these people escape into their 12th House through drugs, alcohol or prescription medication. Many live alone, deliberately isolating themselves from others. This way they can manage the comings and goings in their life much better. It is a way of taking command of their life. It reduces their contact with people who are generally their main stressors.

I am talking of those people who spend long periods of time in their deep unconscious. These natives have Inner Planets and/or the Luminaries in their 12th House, or sometimes they will have the natural Ruler of the 12th, Neptune, conjunct a Luminary or their 1st or 12th House Cusp. Any of these scenarios will manifest similarly to having the Sun or the Moon in the 12th House. When personal Planets are conjunct Neptune, the natural Ruler of this House, it can become a focal point in the personality.

These natives respond to counseling extremely well, as long as they turn up. Many will attend a few sessions then say, *"I am feeling so much better now, thank you,"* and stop coming. They may need more therapy and usually return in a few months when things start to fall apart again.

This is the reason I deliberately go very slowly. I ensure that I build and establish a basis for them to trust. I know that when things do fall apart, they will drop in for a few sessions to chat. This on and off counseling is what works best for these natives. It's the most efficient way for them to gain control over a process that they normally cannot manage - interacting with another person.

I have found that those with a 12th House focus aren't afraid to talk about their problems or even do some in-depth therapy, but they get exhausted quickly, sometimes it drains them too much to commit to ongoing therapy.

I do not want you to think that 12th House people need psychotherapy, not at all, they manage just as well as everyone else. They can resort to hiding more than others, though. Dreaming and escaping, avoiding other people is so much safer and uses less energy than any other form of therapy. It can sometimes be called the House of Fatigue. These natives use so much of their psychic energy just to cope with and manage daily life, that they become exhausted.

Those who can swim in these waters are the masters of life. They need a lot of support though to stay engaged and avoid escaping into addiction or running away to isolate themselves. The masters of the 12th House tend to have good support networks. Secure relationships become the gatekeepers to the outside world. This guards against disruption in their lives.

Their sentinels protect the 12th House master from stressful people and situations. This is probably the best scenario for a dominant 12th House person. Find someone you trust to manage your affairs while you take up meditation, religious studies, painting, music or writing.

Archetypal Meditation - 12th House

My Meditation: I have Sagittarius on my 12th House Cusp and no Planets inside; it is a bit like Pluto's Cave. The 12th House, too, has always been a cave for me. I find that it is also a holding stage for Planets before they transit into the 1st House for rebirth. These Planets try to resolve psychological issues of the past in the 12th House before entering the 1st. It is as if they needed to let go of their baggage and get ready for a fresh start in a new cycle.

This cave reminds me of the cave of the one-eyed Cyclops, when Odysseus and his crew escaped by wearing sheep skins, pretending to be sheep. I can feel what the men around me want; they are planning an escape. Sagittarius, the archer, is quite adventurous, it seems he has become Odysseus in this meditation.

The cave smells of body odour, the sweat of hard working men crowded together. Cyclops is sitting quietly, guarding the cave entrance, he is eating and not bothered by us. Sagittarius is our leader, we wait for him to direct our escape. The excitement and fear is palpable; I can smell it.

Odysseus looks like Pan, the Goat God. My Chiron and Pluto also take this form sometimes. He has a short beard, small horns and cloven hooves; he is a satyr. I know him well.

"You are trapped, and you will remain so as long as you rely on someone else to organise your rescue." He speaks softly. I know that, I have learned not to count on anyone else these days. "True, but this is your 12th House, your Underworld, not Pluto's underworld which you know so well. This is where your dreams come from, and where you store unresolved issues from your past. It isn't like Pluto's Cave where you can change things with your chi and kundalini."

I'm not sure I like that much, I thought I had a handle on the 12th

House, but it seems that I don't. After all I work with people with unresolved issues from their past every day. I take them into their 12th House to rescue their inner selves, children and adults. It's what I do best. I also do it for myself, not well enough it seems, according to Pan/Sagittarius/Odysseus.

"You are close, but not quite close enough." He smiles with delight, as if he was about to announce the punch line of a joke. "Dreams arise from your 12th House - dreaming, you are a dreamer, work more with your dreams. I know that you program them, we want you to do more of this programming, layering and structuring. Remember, you do this every day, you know what to do, let us help."

I am not frightened to do this 12th House work, I just need my sleep! "OK," I decide to negotiate. "I'll let you work with me from 3 a.m. to 6 a.m. only. I really do need my sleep so no inner dreamwork before that time." Sagittarius smiles, he is fine with that, in fact, very pleased because he knew I would say that. "How do you want me to do this?" I ask him.

"Before you fall asleep, program us to do your inner work between the hours of 3 a.m. and 6 a.m., it's that simple, but be specific with what you want done. We can't do anything without your permission, you already know that." Yes, that's true, I advise my clients every day, ask and you will receive. "Don't forget that it also requires practice, if you don't practice this every night, using the same routine, it won't work." Sagittarius fades, but I am stuck in Cyclops' cave… tonight, I plan to find my own way out, what an exciting adventure that will be!

Postscript: that evening I programmed my dreams as instructed. What a night it was, amazing dreams about my past, they were all healing and insightful. I am going to do this as often as I can. It is certainly fascinating and extremely important for a therapist to do his own therapy.

Chart Interpretations:

Barack Obama - has Capricorn on his 12th House suggesting that the qualities of reliability, structure, organization and dependability may be hidden. Therefore, he may feel less inclined to be structured, or these qualities agitate or interfere with his internal harmony.

A Capricorn 12th House with Jupiter and Saturn in it suggests that these two Planets are hardly allowed expression in his psyche. These are two very powerful Planets, and the fact that they are buried in the 12th House can bring on some issues related to their specific characteristics.

Saturn is order and structure, he likes things to be well constructed from sturdy material and on solid ground. If those foundations are not strong, he will knock them down and force the native to rebuild them properly. That's why he is so devastating when he transits our Houses and Planets.

Jupiter is expansion, he loves to travel and study, he delights in adventure and parties. These two in the 12th House suggest that Barack Obama sometimes fails to set proper foundations and that he is working when he should be playing. Stifling these natural urges leads to illness; so this is an excellent opportunity for some great archetypal meditations.

Hilary Clinton - notice that four of her Planets are in her 12th House. This suggests that Hilary may struggle to fully engage with her sensitive Sun, her self-esteem and self-worth; or with Chiron, her wounded self. Venus, her sense of love and beauty is also hiding; and so is her clever Mercury, her mind. These are all focal points in the dark 12th House. All this indicates that Hilary has had to work twice as hard as anyone else to achieve what she has in life.

One of these Planets, Venus, we know a lot about: her husband,

Bill, had an affair with his staffer, Monica. It was on the news all over the globe. A hidden Venus would act as if it didn't touch her, though betrayal and abandonment would describe well what she must have felt.

With these powerful Planets placed in the 12th House, she could not rise to the occasion and reject him. Self-worth, self-esteem, love and being wounded are all hidden and cause suppressed mental stress when pushed deeper. She has had to continually bottle these feelings up to cope with the pain. It was easier for her this way because she lives in the 12th House of the unconscious, she's used to working harder than everyone else. That 12th House shows us just how far she has had to go to cope and to survive the torture of abandonment.

Do you know the story of the fox and the scorpion? One day, a fox was about to jump into the river to swim across to the other side when a scorpion came up to him and asked him for a ride. *"No, you're a scorpion and you'll sting me. I will be paralyzed, I'll stop swimming and I'll drown,"* said the fox.

"No I won't, I promise I won't sting you. I want to get to the other side of the river just like you do. If I sting you, we'll both drown," replied the scorpion.

The fox thought about it for a moment then agreed. Why would the scorpion sting him if he knew they would both die? *"OK, climb onto my back and I'll carry you across the river."* said the fox.

When they reached the middle of the river, the fox felt a stinging sensation on his neck. *"What did you just do? You idiot, you stung me and now we'll both drown,"* cried the fox in despair. *"You promised not to sting me, why did you do it?"* he said.

"I am a scorpion, it's in my nature," came the scorpion's reply as

he was sinking into the river clinging to the paralyzed fox.

The lesson of Scorpio on the 12th Cusp is its sting, it is highlighted when too much emphasis is placed on this Sign. It will manifest its pain in the House it sits in. Remember the Scorpion's nature: in the parable above, as in real life, a Scorpion stings whether this causes suffering to itself or not. That's the challenge a Scorpio faces, to overcome its instinctual urge to self-destruct. In Hilary's case, her strength of character has stopped her 12th House (and Ascendant) Scorpion from harming her.

Justin Bieber - interestingly, he also has a loaded, Scorpionic 12th House with Jupiter, the North Node and Pluto inside. These three Planets draw the Signs they rule into the 12th House with them. Pluto rules Scorpio, which is on the Cusp of the 1st and 12th Houses, indicating that Justin tends to hide his Ascendant (his real self) from the public, nobody really knows who he is, and it is nobody's business anyway. Jupiter rules Sagittarius, intercepted inside the 1st House, which magnifies what Pluto has been doing, bringing the 1st House into his 12th. We could say that it is almost impossible to know the real Justin Bieber. He has so many facets, and most of them he wears on the inside.

Taylor Swift Facebook Time - Taylor has Sagittarius on the Cusp of her 12th House and her Sun is inside. The Sun therefore draws Leo, the Sign it rules, into the 12th House. Leo sits on the 8th House Cusp suggesting that her psychological and occult interests lie in the deep unknown of the 12th House. She could easily tap into her 12th House, perhaps by learning to meditate, practicing yoga, tai chi, etc. Her Sun is also hidden in this House, which indicates that her father was absent; he either didn't live with her or he was emotionally unavailable.

Taylor Swift Twitter Time - this chart has Cancer on the 12th House Cusp. This is an emotional Sign and may suggest that she sometimes struggles to access her emotional self. It can also imply that she often wrestles with emotions, sometimes breaking through her defenses from the deep unconscious. There are no Planets in this House, but its ruler, the Moon, is in her 11th, so this House is also involved in her inner conflicts.

12th House Planetary Ruler	Neptune
Sign Correspondence	Pisces
Angles/Qualities	Cadent
Elements / Trinities	Water / Psychological
Health	Psychological health, the feet and toes
Keywords	subconscious, higher self, skeletons, hidden strengths and weaknesses, imprisonment, secrets, spirituality and the deepest psyche

Psychotherapy in the 12th House

An older man, I shall call him Guy, attended psychotherapy after a breakdown. He was one of the meekest, quietest and most gentle of men I have ever worked with – a true gentleman. He clearly demonstrated extremely strong Piscean characteristics. He must have had indicators of Pisces in his chart such as Neptune conjunct his Ascendant, the Sun or the Moon, or had a stellium in the 12th House itself. He also may have had the Sun and Moon or at least one of them in the 12th House.

I was right, he had Taurus Ascendant with the Sun, Mercury, Venus and the Moon, in his enormous 12th House. This stellium in the 12th makes him extremely Piscean. This can be said in another way: he was a 12th House person, or 12th House dominant.

This fellow was very gentle; he also had a special charm, I easily warmed to his unique personality.

After a short discussion of his past, it turned out that he had several university degrees and postgraduate qualifications, he was extremely intelligent. One piece of information that really got me thinking was that he had experienced significant bullying through most of his high school years.

There was one particular incident that was key to my psychotherapy decisions: he believed that he had killed his grandmother.

She had tripped over him in the garden and was knocked unconscious. He was only four years old. She died soon afterwards, he blamed himself. To cement this belief of guilt into his deep unconscious, his best friend died a year later. Death is an intriguing life theme that corresponds to the 12th as the last House in the cycle of the zodiac.

These two deep and traumatic experiences led me to begin depth psychotherapy. He was about to enter his 12th House and rescue those tortured inner selves. My reasoning was to get him started in therapy as soon as possible to prevent self-harming.

I talked about the inner world and that he was going to meet his inner self. I explained that this was a part of his psyche that represented his emotions; it was his Emotional Self. He sat and nodded woodenly. I remarked that he didn't seem to be running out of the room with his hands in the air, screaming in terror. He half smiled, it looked like he was going to cry, or perhaps laugh. And that's how he started an episode of his life that changed everything for him.

Our first hypnotherapy session found him at an old, collapsing stone fort, high up in the Pyrenees. His Inner Self was standing beside him. He started to cry, his eyes closed tight, still in trance. When he eventually opened his eyes, he told me what had happened.

"He said that he was angry with me; he was really angry. I felt ashamed; I had failed him. He told me I had to change or else I will die." His face contorted and more tears streamed down.

When he asked his Inner Self what he needed to do to change, his Self replied, *"You need to be honest and show your real self."* They hugged and then he took Guy to the walls of the derelict fort and handed him a sledgehammer. Together, they began to break down the walls.

At our next session, I asked him if he had been doing his meditations. He said that he had, diligently. He was even more keen to become the person he now felt he could be. He said that he was confused, he didn't understand what was going on inside him, but he wanted to do more therapy.

It was time to challenge his belief that he had killed his grandmother. Whether true or not, he needed to revisit and rescue that tortured four-year-old.

"Let yourself feel comfortable in your chair. As you breathe out, relax, and go deeper and deeper, until you find your inner self, that little four-year-old you, sitting in the garden, playing. Your grandmother is there too, waiting for you." I guided him to relax and to meet his younger self. I had explained previously that he was going back in time as his 60-year-old self, desperate to change his past.

He saw his little self and gave him a hug. Then he went over to his grandmother who was sitting at the garden bench with a pot of tea on a round table. She was waiting for him and poured a cup of tea for him. They talked for quite a long time, I waited until he was done. He cried when he came back. Not tears of sadness, but of relief.

"We sat down together, she had a cup of tea waiting for me, we chatted, Grandma and me. She said that I hadn't killed her at all, she told me that she died a year or so later, of old age. She explained that she worked on the family farm with my grandfather and those were very difficult times. Most days she wouldn't eat, she gave her food to her children because they were so poor. This was what had slowly killed her, complications from years of malnutrition." He sat quietly, we talked about his grandmother. He had no idea what she was talking about, but he felt that it might be true.

At our next session he told me that he had confirmation from his family that his Grandma died a year or so after her accident. She died of exactly what she had told him in trance. He was quietly excited about this confirmation.

A few weeks later we met again for his therapy session. He told me that he had been working diligently in his inner world. His older Inner Self took him down a set of stairs to a dungeon-like room below the fort. In the middle of the room, there was a locked treasure chest, but he couldn't open it.

We did some inner work with his teenage younger self and helped him deal with some bullies at school. This was very hard because his teenage self initially rejected this old man's help, he didn't want to be near him. Everything changed when Guy stood up to the bullies and they ran away. Then the teenager decided to relax a little.

Guy then led his teenage-self aside and began to teach him martial arts. His younger self was very excited. At first he wouldn't talk, but after doing the martial arts exercises, he became quite chatty and funny.

At the next session, Guy sat down and told me that he was quite confused because of what had happened one morning when lying in bed on the weekend.

"I was lying in bed, without thinking about anything, just sort of awake, when an ancient, Roman looking man appeared, very clearly, right next to my bed." He smiled and his face crinkled, I couldn't tell if he was going to cry or laugh. *"Before I could say anything the man said, 'I am Augustine, read my book,' and then he disappeared."*

So he got up to do a search on the internet and he immediately bought Augustine's autobiography in an ebook format. *"He was a wild man in his youth, he did a lot of bad things. His attitudes were much like mine."* Guy went on, *"I haven't read all of it yet but I think I know what he is saying to me."*

I didn't push for any further information; I could see on his face and feel in his tone that there was more to come. *"I went back to the fort and we went to the treasure chest. I could open it this time. You know the Monsters Inc movie, there is this little green monster?"* I nodded. *"He jumped out of the chest and started running around and around in the room. I had no idea what to do."*

He told me that his Inner Self laughed with glee when Mike Wasowski from Monsters Inc. popped out from the treasure chest.

I then asked him to sit back in his chair, I put on some natural river sounds that he enjoyed during relaxation. I took him back to his cave and suggested that he ask this monster if he represented a part of his psyche.

"I went into the cave, they were still there. When I asked the green dude 'what part of me do you represent?' my Inner Self said, 'You don't know? It's you, he represents you. He wants to get out into the Sun and live.' But I'm worried that he will create havoc in my life if I let him out. I am frightened that he'll make a fool of me." Guy had a worried frown on his face, once again I wasn't sure if he was going to cry or laugh.

Guy and I talked for a while about these events and what he might do next. I guided him back into his cave and he let his green monster run up the stairs into the sunlight. Guy followed him.

When he came out of trance he said, *"When I got to the top of the stairs, there was a crowd of people waiting for me. They were all so happy, my grandfathers, great-grandfathers and grandmothers… other friends and family who had passed on were there too. Many I didn't even recognise."* He had that expression again, this time tears began to stream down his cheeks.

One of them, who introduced himself as James, said to him, *"We are so happy for you, now you are who you are. You could never be as bad as I was, though."* Guy didn't know who James was, but he thought that maybe he was one of his great-great-great grandfathers. He wanted to find out what James was talking about, but he needed a plan.

This gentleman was now walking straight, he no longer stooped as he had been when he came for therapy a few months earlier. As he left, I shook his hand, *"Welcome back to life, Guy."* He had that funny smile, again. It slowly turned into a real, full-faced smile.

Perhaps I will finish this amazing story at another time, or maybe I don't need to because you have already guessed the outcome.

Point to Remember: all Signs are exactly 30° (degrees) in every zodiac Sign, but the size of the Houses can vary according to geographic longitude and latitude, the House System used and the time of year. When the eastern horizon reaches 29° it is only 1°, or 4 minutes, away from 30° - which is the end of that Sign and the beginning of the next.

Guy – 12th House
Natal Chart

The Houses as a Life Story

1st - birth, delivery and the experiences of the first two years of life, Freud's oral stage and forming attachments outside the self

2nd - from two years of age to four years, learning about security, movement, the physical body and its limitations, Freud's anal stage and potty training

3rd - the early school years, learning and communicating, exploring the world

4th - around the 7th year of life when the native becomes an individual, it is family conditioning and primary or junior school

5th - teenage years, the native learns about self-expression, individuality, identity, creativity and hobbies, discovers sex and makes friends

6th - the 20's, the native becomes aware of commitments and responsibility, takes on a job, the end of childhood and the beginning of adulthood

7th - the start of adult life, the native forms legal relationships, this stage is similar to the first year of marriage. This is when we enter the public arena and through marriage and business, we announce that we are part of society

8th - late 20's to 30's, the native has a young family. Becoming a parent is a turning point when we return to family and recognise how our own parents felt. Parenthood is a crisis, it is both a reversal and recognition, we have to deal with the power we have to transform our evolving infant

9th - the children grow up and leave home, and the native is freed from the pressures and duties of raising a family. They begin to explore the philosophies of life they had put on hold. This period is another coming of age

10th - the native reaches the big 40th birthday, it is the peak of their career. Their ambitions have been realised at last, and they are reaping the harvest of all those years of hard work. Alternatively, they come to terms with their failings, detach themselves from society's expectations and establish their own sense of worth and achievement.

11th - the 50's and the 60's, the native is past the peak and dreaming of the future for themselves and humanity. They become philosophical and are able to express and share their wisdom with their grandchildren

12th - this is the last House, the completion of a cycle, death is around the corner and the native is able to look upon life in a holistic way. They also have glimpses of the future after their earthly life and they are preparing for rebirth into the 1st House.

Planetary Patterns in the Houses

Stellium - a grouping of four or more Planets in the same House or Sign. It emphasizes that particular House and/or Sign. Astrologers will sometimes include asteroids like Chiron, and the North Node. A stellium in a House is sometimes called a 'loaded House'. Similarly, a stellium in a Sign can be called a 'loaded Sign'.

Many astrologers will call a group of three Planets a 'mini-stellium'. It's not really a stellium but it helps us understand where the native focuses their energies. A stellium shows that there is psychological impact on the native in that particular Sign or House. It is a focal point for their psychological, spiritual, emotional and physical energy.

Barack Obama has a stellium in Leo: Mercury, Sun, Uranus and the North Node, they are split between the 6th and the 7th Houses. He also has a stellium in his 7th House: Uranus, the North Node, Pluto and Mars. This set of four Planets in Leo shows HOW he expresses these Planets, and the 7th House stellium adds emphasis on WHERE they are expressed. The 7th House is other people, his partner Michelle and his intimate friends. It also sheds light on his constituency, as this is also reflected in the 7th House.

Hilary Clinton has a stellium in her 12th House, in Scorpio. This adds enormous power to her 12th House, and it also focuses her attention on her psychological strengths and weaknesses. We could say that Hilary's 12th House is an intense and passionate focal point for her psychological development. So is her mini-stellium in her 9th House of learning, morals and law, but with a touch of adventure, nurturing and travel.

Justin Bieber has a stellium in his 3rd House in Aquarius and Pisces: Mercury, Mars, Saturn and Sun. This indicates that it is important for him to communicate in a simple and effective manner, particularly with young people. He also has a mini-stellium in his 12th House suggesting that he has some work to do on addressing his emotional needs.

Taylor Swift, in her **Facebook Time** chart, has a five-planet stellium in the 1st House, four of the Planets are in Capricorn. We would say that Taylor has a Capricorn stellium in her 1st House. It consists of Mercury, Neptune, Saturn, Venus and the North Node. It shows that she is focused on being the one and only, the best and the first at all costs. We also find a Cancer mini-stellium with the Moon, Jupiter and Chiron across the Cusp of her 7th House.

In Taylor's **Twitter Time** chart, we see a stellium of five Planets in her 5th House of creativity and friendship. They are slightly different than the ones in her Facebook Time chart because of the time change. They are the Sun, Uranus, Mercury, Neptune and Saturn. The mini-stellium is in her 11th House of hopes, dreams and wishes. Her Twitter Time chart sure looks more like a performer's chart! I am starting to think that her Facebook time is incorrect and that her Twitter time is probably the right one.

House Groupings

There are several ways to organise Houses into certain categories, I will only mention a few here, those I have found informative. These groupings are ways to get a quick snapshot of an individual by looking at what Planets reside in which House. We do this by placing the Houses into groups. We also look at the influence Rulerships have on a Planet. The more Planets in a House or Group of Houses (House Groupings), the more informative this is. For example a stellium, like **Justin Bieber's** in the 3rd House, is a very important pattern that we need to fully understand to properly delineate his chart.

Geographical House Divisions

Geographical divisions are very general descriptions and are easily overruled by other factors in the chart. They can be useful, but only for a general feel for the chart, requires seven or more Planets to influence the native.

Northern - Houses 1 to 6 - subjective and avoidant, the native shows tendencies to withdraw from others, enjoys working and operating successfully away from the public eye.

Southern - Houses 7 to 12 - objective, optimistic and embracing, the native enjoys plunging into life, they are happy, gregarious, enjoy public recognition and praise.

Eastern - Houses 10 to 3 - controlling and leading, a strong presentation and bearing, the native likes to take charge and they make their own breaks in life. The 12th House may weaken this tendency if overemphasized.

Western - Houses 4 to 9 - impressionable and pessimistic, often wanting others to do everything for them, a weakness which may be seen as being overly gullible. Easily influenced by others but very charming and social, people love to invite them to parties.

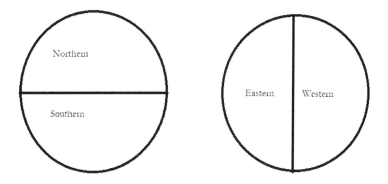

The Four Elemental Houses - also called Trinities or Triplicities

This House division corresponds to the four Elements of the twelve zodiac Signs and require four or more Planets to have a strong influence.

Fire Houses -1, 5 & 9 - Life / Personal - these Houses represent your vitality and self-expression through your individual creativity and actions. These people are idealists, adventurers and local heroes who show us that it is possible to be spiritual and human at the same time. An over-emphasis on these Houses can lead to its negative characteristics: narcissistic, self-centred and childish behaviour. No longer the heroes we worship, they can become the bullies we fear.

Earth Houses - 2, 6 & 10 - Wealth / Work - these people are interested in and concerned with material possessions. They are dedicated to completing a task and are reliable in work and play. They are not necessarily money-oriented, but they understand the usefulness and power of financial and material security. Often they are the ones who hold the community together through their wise use of time and energy. These natives teach us how to go about creating security in our lives. If this element dominates the chart, it is possible that its negative characteristics will show, such as being lazy, indulgent, greedy, hoarding and accumulating possessions at the expense of others. Once idolised for their sensible lifestyles and work ethics, they become the target of unhappy tenants, students and staff.

Air Houses - 3, 7 & 11 - Relationship / Social -these natives are people-oriented, they need to connect and share, Facebook is filled with Air Signs. Often seen at parties, talking on the phone and at the negotiating table, these people may whither if they don't have someone to talk to. They are communicators, we can learn a lot from them about planning, strategy and relating to one another for the betterment of humanity. An unhealthy focus on these House qualities can lead to worry, meaningless meetings, endless texts and grandiose thinking. We respect our leaders who exhibit good communication skills, but when they fail us, we feel manipulated.

Water Houses - 4, 8 & 12 - Psychic / Psychological - a focus on these Houses shows emotional sensitivity. These natives may benefit from some form of counseling or mentoring to help them understand and cope with their sensitivity and psychic ability. As said before, sensitive/psychic people often dwell in their inner world and require grounding. This is often through specific meditation techniques and any form of physical, mental and emotional discipline. These are our inspirational dreamers. Too much emphasis on these Houses can lead to an over-sensitive individual who requires constant reassurance and nurturing. They can experience severe mood swings, but usually it is directed inwards, at themselves. These natives often quietly self-destruct; they become recluses, they are not the noisemakers of the other elemental Houses.

Barack Obama - has a slight emphasis on the Air Houses; namely, four Planets in his 7th House. This is standard fare for a politician. They need charisma and an outgoing personality, they have to be able to work with and empower others. Politics is definitely his game.

Hilary Clinton - has four Planets in Fire Houses, no Planets in Earth Houses, two Planets in Air Houses and six in Water Houses - she has an emphasis on the Psychological Water Houses.

Justin Bieber - has one Planet in Fire Houses, two Planets in Earth Houses, five in Air Houses and four Planets in Water Houses - his Air Houses are dominant.

Taylor Swift Facebook Time - there are five Planets in Fire Houses, three in Earth Houses, two Planets in Air Houses and two in Water Houses - her Fire element is highlighted.

Taylor Swift Twitter Time - there are five Planets in Fire Houses, one in an Earth House, four in Air and two Planets in Water Houses - the Fire element has the most emphasis.

Angles - Qualities or Volumes

This House division requires a majority of Planets in the particular Houses to be activated. Astrologers have used this House division quite extensively. Michel Gauquelin (author of *Cosmic Influences on Human Behaviour,* 1973) was a French statistician who found that Planets closest to the angles of the chart had a more powerful effect on the personality than anywhere else in the chart. For example, Mars was strong for athletes, Jupiter for actors and Saturn for scientists.

Astrologers traditionally held the four Angles (1st, 4th, 7th and 10th Houses) as the strongest Houses regardless of where a Planet sat inside them. Gauquelin found, after extensive research of thousands of famous people in France, that Planets within 8° applying (coming closer in an anticlockwise direction) to the Angles were the strongest.

Therefore any Planet approaching the 1st, 4th, 7th or 10th House Cusp (Angle) is stronger than if it was leaving the House Cusp (separating) or in the middle of the House.

Angular Houses - 1, 4, 7 & 10 - form a cross through the chart and can indicate those who are inspired and motivated to achieve. They are driven by any Planets in close aspect to the Cusps. They sometimes prefer to live for today rather than put off till tomorrow, *"I want it now!"*

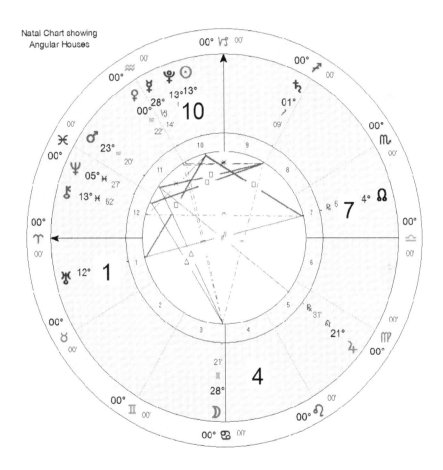

Natal Chart showing Angular Houses

Succedent Houses - 2, 5, 8 & 11 - indicate a person who leads a more grounded existence. They can plan and organise themselves for tomorrow, but may not be quick enough to respond to today's opportunities. They tend to live in the future, *"Everything is set and ready for tomorrow, why bother with today's problems?"*

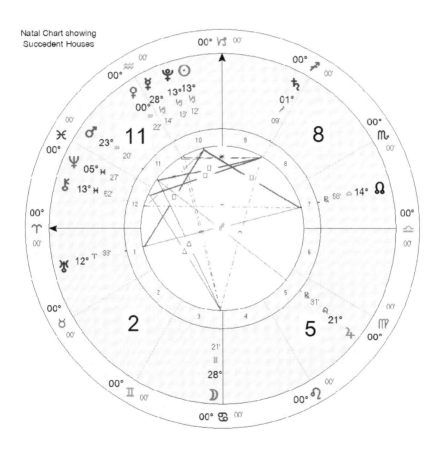

Natal Chart showing Succedent Houses

Cadent Houses - 3, 6, 9 & 12 - for these natives, adaptation is the keyword. They are not very dynamic but they can cope with the stresses of life well, though they do tend to worry and live in the past. *"I shouldn't have done it. I wish I could turn back the clock"*

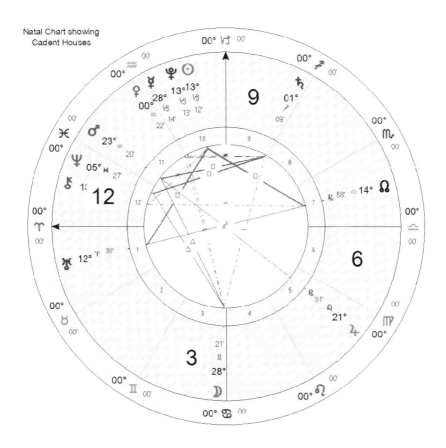

Natal Chart showing Cadent Houses

171

Barack Obama - has six Planets in Angular, one in Succedent, five in Cadent Houses - he has an emphasis on the Angular Houses. This suggests a self-made man, driven to get things moving and make them happen.

Hilary Clinton - has three Planets in Angular, two in Succedent, seven in Cadent Houses - her Cadent Houses are stressed, indicating that she is able to finish things with a flair.

Justin Bieber - has one Planet in Angular, three in Succedent, eight in Cadent Houses - he has an emphasis on his Cadent Houses showing that he is more prone to finishing projects than starting something new.

Taylor Swift Facebook Time - there are seven Planets in Angular, one in Succedent, four in Cadent Houses - she has an emphasis on her Angular Houses: she is a self-starter and she is good at starting things but may struggle to keep them going.

Taylor Swift Twitter Time - there are three Planets in Angular, eight in Succedent, one in Cadent Houses - she has focus on her Succedent Houses: she is persistent, she gets her teeth fixed into a task and won't let go.

The importance of the four Angular Houses - Michel Gauquelin

Astrologers have found that Planets within 8° either side of the angular Cusps (1st, 4th, 7th and 10th Cusp lines) are very powerful teachers. This is especially important for Planets closest to the Ascendant (1st Cusp) and the Midheaven (10th Cusp).

All Planets in Angular Houses are strong, stronger than in any other House, with some exceptions. According to Gauquelin, the most powerful Planets are those within 8° applying (moving towards, in an anti-clockwise direction) to the Angular Cusp but still in the Cadent Houses. I have found that any Planet within about 5° either side of an Angular Cusp is extremely strong, the 8° applying rule is a very good guide. Explore your own chart and see what you think.

In **Barack Obama's chart,** we see that his Sun is conjunct (next to) and applying his 7th House Cusp; it is only 6° away from this Cusp. In other words, the Sun is within Gauquelin's sphere of influence. This makes the Sun more influential on the 7th House affairs. It is almost a 7th House Planet, it has such an influence there because of this close placement. His Moon is just over 4° past the 4th House Cusp. The Moon is separating (moving away from) the Cusp going deeper into the House. This, too, places an emphasis on the 4th House Cusp and the Moon, but it is not quite as powerful as an applying aspect.

In some ways, we could say that an applying Planet stresses the House Cusp, while a separating Planet emphasises the Planet itself.

Hilary Clinton - using Gauquelin's criteria, we can see that Mercury is 1° applying to her Ascendant, indicating that her mental faculties are foremost. Venus is just within the 8° range, this suggests that her social charm shines through, too. I would go one step further and say that her North Node, separating from her 7th House Cusp, is also very strong. Next, I would look at any Planets at the Angles, the Moon is in the 4th House and Jupiter is in the 1st. All these Planets are very powerful forces impacting her psyche.

Justin Bieber - only Venus in the 4th is in an Angular House, but have you noticed the Sun applying to the 4th Cusp from the 3rd House? It's within 6° of the Cusp, so it is very strong and activating the 4th House. Pluto and the North Node are applying to the Ascendant from the 12th House, 1° and 3° away, so these are also very powerful and they activate his Ascendant with their particular energies.

Taylor Swift Facebook Time - that 1st House is loaded, her Planets within are all strong, but have you spotted the strongest ones? Uranus is 4° applying to the Ascendant from the 12th House, that is Gauquelin's special placement. Then there are Jupiter and the Moon applying from the 6th to the 7th Cusp, also very powerful.

Taylor Swift Twitter Time - her Planets in Angular Houses are Pluto and Mars in the 4th. This shows strong family and childhood issues, weaknesses and strengths, The North Node on her 7th House Cusp is very strong: it is only 2° away from the Cusp.

Have you decided which birth time is most suitable for her? I am still not entirely sure because I don't know her in person, but I lean towards the Twitter birth time. What do you think?

Houses as Psychological Defences

The Four Elements of Earth, Air, Fire and Water are extremely powerful indicators of distinct personality styles, both as strengths and weaknesses. They have been expanded upon by such talented psychological astrologers as Liz Greene, Howard Sasportas, Stephen Arroyo and Glenn Perry. When analysing the Houses, astrologers can extract a lot of information on the native's personality by examining the Elemental Defences associated with each House.

Both a planetary emphasis or a lack of emphasis on an Element has the potential to create a Psychological Defence. The native can become overly defensive in that Element due to the many factors described below.

The Four House Elements as Psychological Defences

- which have also been called 'Defence Mechanisms' provide essential barriers to protect us from the harsh realities of the outside world. They can sometimes put us into survival-mode. Everyone has them, but if we use them too frequently, they can become a real problem. They start to cause trouble when when they serve as barriers and we withdraw behind them at the first sign of inner conflict.

In extreme cases, we can end up struggling to fully or openly participate in the world around us. Astrologers see our client's defences in the Planets, Signs, Houses, the Ascendant and the chart Signature that highlights one or more Elements in their natal chart.

We all have defences but not everyone has a dominant Element. If so, we work backwards from the Planets, chart Signature, House emphasis, Ascendant and the most aspected Planet until an Element begins to show dominance. We need to be careful because there may be more than one. Defences work closely with Jung's Complexes and Projections.

Water House Defence - defends against abandonment, betrayal, neglect, rejection and loneliness by attaching to others and/or to love objects.

The famous psychiatrist Dr Sigmund Freud explained that our first reflex at birth is to suckle at our mother's breast. He called this the Oral Stage of PsychoSexual development. Feelings of warmth, attachment, belonging, love, joy, nurturing, satisfaction and fulfilment come from this initial experience. When the child is weaned and the breast is withdrawn, it can set off a need for a substitute breast such as a toy, food, a dummy/pacifier, thumb sucking, a nanny, cigarettes, etc. These substitutes displace the real breast.

If the infant's emotional (Water) needs are not met, they can become fixated at the Water stage of development, they will seek substitutes: other people or objects.

The oral reflex is a natural phenomenon, it is a most powerful experience for the newborn. It's much like our first encounter with a stranger, our first impression lasts the longest. Imagine that the breast is withdrawn before the child is fulfilled and satisfied, a yearning begins, a yearning that can manifest as a defence.

A Water Defence is seen when a native experiences abandonment or betrayal by a loved one. When their relationship breaks up, they feel loss and their grief is greater than would normally be expected. I see abandonment issues every day in my practice, it provides therapists with most of their work.

Water strengths include the ability to empathise with others, to feel compassion and to engage fully in nurturing. Healers of all kinds have a strong Water element. We also find them in the creative arts: writers, media professionals, visual artists and musicians. They expand our world through their vision.

Astrologers find Water Defences when the Sun, or more commonly the Moon, is in a Water sign, a Water House or in poor aspect with the outer planets, Neptune, Chiron or Pluto. To find a Water Defence in the chart, we need to look for a poorly aspected luminary in a Water sign or in conjunction with an outer planet in the 4th, 8th or 12th House. Sometimes this can be seen in the 7th House if there is a Water dominance in that House.

Earth House Defence - defends against the insecurity of change by exerting control over one's possessions and physical environment. Freud called this the Anal Stage of PsychoSexual development. It uses power struggles with authority figures, hoarding and collecting, not releasing control of their possessions.

This is the defence that develops at around the time of potty or toilet training. The issue is one of controlling the physical world. Freud puts this stage at around the time when the child discovers that they can control their flow of urine and faeces. These biological areas are also erogenous zones that are stimulated when excreting.

When the child discovers that they enjoy these experiences, they want to be in control. However, it is the mother who puts them on the potty and she makes them stay there until it is done. Mother is in charge and she claims the actual product of control. This can set up a power conflict between authority (mother, father or nanny) and the child.

This defence is a power conflict with anyone with authority who has the power to remove the native's control over their pleasure-giving possessions. This resistance is projected onto the school teacher, police, neighbour and anyone else who tells them what to do and when to do it.

The child wants to be in charge of everything that brings pleasure, be it the toilet, bath, playing with toys or having fun with their friends. As they grow older they control and collect other gratifying things such as money, houses, cars, partners, lovers, etc.

This defence can become destructive when they fall in love and start dating. The Earth person learns to control the giving and withholding of another crucial product: affection. This creates a battleground in the marriage and I will often see them for counseling.

Earth strengths include the incredible stamina to see a task through, no matter how challenging it may be. Think of those postmen who set out no matter what the weather is like, and do their job in rain, hail or sunshine. When something involves perseverance, it is those with a strong Earth element who will have it done. They are reliable and dependable in their desire to complete a task with maximum efficiency.

Earth Defences are seen in the Luminaries in Earth signs or Houses, and poor aspects to Venus (in Taurus), Saturn and Mercury (in Virgo). For psychologists and counselors, a Planetary stellium in an Earth House will help you examine this defence in a therapy session.

Air House Defence - defends against emotions, reality, confusion, ambivalence and restricted freedom of expression. It denies that anything is wrong, it dissociates and escapes into fantasy to avoid facing emotional issues, comes up with intellectual explanations, resorts to denial and magical thinking.

We leave Dr Sigmund Freud here and we now stick with the defenses used by other astrologer psychologists. This is called the Denial Stage by Liz Greene and Howard Sasportas.

Air Defences seek to dissociate and adopt an intellectual mindset to avoid painful emotional situations and feelings. They cut off their emotions and prefer to engage only with their conscious, rational mind. They have great difficulty expressing how they feel, they are most comfortable talking about love and affection, not experiencing or demonstrating them.

The Air Defences seek counseling when they become stuck inside their heads. These clients are unable to acknowledge and face their feelings. This defence appears to be the worst of all the problems that I see in my practice. They think to avoid feeling. It becomes so powerful that it invades their everyday mind and prevents them falling asleep. It is probably the most common cause of disturbed sleep in our culture.

I often ask my clients if they have 'racing negative thoughts'. Once this is identified, I can help them disengage their busy conscious mind and direct them to talk about what is really going on in their lives. This involves a complex series of therapeutic process including self hypnosis, meditation, basic relaxation activities and biofeedback. Air Defences are very difficult to treat, but they react very well to the above strategies.

When the Sun or Moon are in Air signs or Houses, it is easy for Air Defences to ignore their emotions. They will deny, rationalise and make logical any emotional issue that arises. There is nothing more powerful than a good argument. The Air Signs use this to avoid real life conflicts whether they are external or internal.

Air strengths include the ability to plan ahead and to fully review past history to predict the future. The Air element dominates our accounting and legal fields; it is their mind that sets them apart from the other elements. They can think around any problem, intuitively solve them without knowing how they did it. They also enter our homes through radio, TV and the social media, people with a strong Air element are everywhere.

You can identify this defence when the Sun and Moon are in Air Signs or Houses, an Air Signature, poor aspects to Mercury (in Gemini), Venus (in Libra) and Uranus. Watch for a predominance of Planets, a stellium, in the 3rd, 7th and 11$_{th}$ Houses.

Fire House Defence - defends against insignificance, inertia, personal meaninglessness, impotence, criticism, vulnerability, humiliation and the feeling of being totally ignored and worthless. It seeks to compete with others for attention, wants to be perceived as special, leans towards narcissism, rivalry, jealousy and envy.

This is called the Oedipal Stage. Liz Greene and Howard Sasportas, in their book *The Development of the Personality*, describe the Greek myth of King Oedipus as a Jungian Complex. The Oedipus Complex, they say, is a Fire Complex that defends the native from becoming overwhelmed by humiliation and guilt, insignificance and inertia. The native competes in one-up-man-ship, seeking attention and recognition. This provides meaning and fulfillment in their lives. Sometimes this involves bullying and fighting to gain recognition.

King Oedipus of ancient Greece unknowingly killed his father and then married his mother. According to psychodynamic theory this is seen as a male child seeking to kill or conquer his father so that he can have his mother all to himself.

Greene and Sasportas explain that the mother is the boy's first love and that his father is an obstacle separating them. The child seeks to manoeuvre and gain power by colluding with the mother to remove the father. We see this in dyads whereby mother and child ally against the father. Once the father is defeated, he becomes 'castrated', impotent and powerless.

Sometimes it is the child who loses and becomes 'castrated' himself. Castration was Freud's way of describing a loss of power, impotence. Whoever loses the battle to gain the mother is overpowered and defeated. I will see this sometimes in my practice with men whose children turn against them, usually after a divorce.

Sometimes a son dominates a needy Water Defence mother, who is unable to gain love and affection in other ways. It's also common in single male child families or a single mother with an only child, a son.

In these cases, the mother may actively collude with the son to castrate the father. Where there is no father, the Fire Defence son may dominate his Water Defensive mother who will interpret his control as affection. I am sure this happens in female child families, where the girl child plots with the father to castrate the mother. I have rarely encountered this phenomenon though. I think the dominant position of the mother as the primary caregiver during infancy is a key factor in these Fire Defences.

To prevent or take revenge for castration, or having castrated the father, the Fire Defensive child can become a narcissist, a bully, who seeks dominion over others.

One of the manifestations of the Fire Defence can be seen in sibling rivalry. The children form dyads and triads, ganging up into pairs and triplets to defeat a common foe, be that another sibling or a parent, etc. I recommend R.D. Laing's *The Divided Self* for more on this.

Fire strengths include the ability to start something new where no opportunities existed even moments before. Everyday is an adventure to people with a strong Fire element. They are seen shining in the sports fields, in the cinema, at parties and in leadership: they love the limelight. Want someone to head up an expedition, or give the keynote address at your next presentation? There is no one more delighted.

Fire Defences are found when there is a focus on Fire Signs, Houses and Planets. The Sun, Mars and Jupiter in the 1st, 5th and 9th House, or the Moon in a Fire Sign or House, for example. Other indicators include a Fire Ascendant or a Fire Signature. Also look for a Planetary Stellium in a Fire Sign or House.

Please note, not all Fire Defences involve castrating the father to dominate the mother. Think of it as a child or adult who seeks to be the centre of attention, exhibit narcissistic behaviour patterns, are selfish, etc.

When there are no strong House element

More often than not, a chart will have elemental balance, no single House or Sign will stand out. If the chart has a deficit in a single Element (or two, even), you need to consider whether this is detrimental to the native or not. Some charts will have three elements in balance and one that is either absent or very weak. In this case, we take note of that element and we can discuss with our client how it may manifest in their life.

The greatest tool we have to promote our personal growth is knowledge. When we identify a particular weakness, we can turn it into a strength. For instance, my weakest element is Air. Nevertheless I have spent most of my life communicating in one form or another.

My strongest element is Fire, yet it can interfere with how I express myself. I work extremely hard on communicating because I know how terrible I am at it.

A Quick Chart Analysis of Elemental Defences

I will sometimes perform a quick analysis of my client's elemental defences in this order:

1. The Luminaries
2. Inner Planets
3. Ascendant and Midheaven
4. Stelliums of three or more Planets in a House
5. Stelliums in Signs
6. Outer Planets

It is the archetypal energies of the personal Planets and points that the native feels most intensely. If I have time, I go deeper and explore the rest of the chart. This procedure has proven to be very useful when I want a quick snapshot of my client's defences.

One of your main goals as an astrologer is to locate those strengths and weaknesses in your client's chart that can be used to maximise their enjoyment and engagement in life. It will benefit them greatly if you can read their elemental defences. If you are also a psychotherapist this can help you develop suitable therapeutic interventions.

Common Defence Mechanisms

Defence mechanisms are programs that run silently and deeply within your unconscious to protect you from harmful memories and sensations. You are generally completely unaware of them. The term 'defence' explains how important they are to your self preservation. When a situation arises that upsets your emotional stability, a defence mechanism is initiated to shut it down. This protects you from experiencing those unpleasant feelings and thoughts. It is not a cure, it is more a means to band-aid the problem until you are ready to deal with its underlying cause.

Denial: You ignore or reject the real situation when you find it too difficult or painful to accept something, *"I don't mind at all that you are working with your ex-wife!"*

Rationalization: You come up with excuses to justify your decisions. *"I can't focus on this new exercise program. I might injure my shoulder and then I can't play bowls."*

Intellectualization: A form of rationalisation but more intellectual. *"My inability to confront my affect failings is a form of intellectual rationalisation."*

Isolation of affect: You are able to intellectualise but not feel the emotion. *"My friend died in a car crash yesterday, I am sure I will miss him. What's for dinner tonight?"*

Reaction Formation: You act in the opposite direction to what you really feel. This happens for instance when you don't like something but don't know how to cope with the consequences of expressing it, *"Wow, a pencil sharpener, what a thoughtful gift, I just love it, just what I needed."*

Projection: You dump onto others what you find unacceptable within yourself. *"I think about cheating on you, so you must be cheating on me."*

Displacement: You redirect your feelings onto someone else or some other object. For instance, instead of confronting a difficult workmate, you take it out on your partner when you get home, *"I can't stand you!"*

Suppression: You defend against your thoughts or feelings about a situation. You push it down so you don't feel it. This is the only conscious defence mechanism. *"I will just keep doing what I am doing and I am sure I will just get over it."*

Regression: You revert back to a previous childhood stage, rather than confront current reality. *"I won't give up my safe, old pillow. I can't fall asleep without it."*

Sublimation: You redirect unacceptable feelings or urges so that they are socially acceptable. *"I just got a job in the prison system, you should see all those angry people, I am really going to enjoy working there."*

Defences are how we manage our unconscious urges, instincts and drives. They are how we hold back our inner dragons. It doesn't free them from their prisons and it doesn't heal them. It merely binds them with a ball and chain to stop them running amok and disturbing our life.

Appendix: Charts & Astrological Symbols and Rulerships

List of illustrations:

Barack Obama, Hilary Clinton, Justin Bieber, Taylor Swift Facebook chart, Taylor Swift Twitter chart, Natal Astrological Chart, the glyphs of the Planets and the Zodiac Signs with Rulerships.

Barack Obama
Male Chart
4 Aug 1961 Fri
7.24 pm AHST +10.00
Honolulu, HI
21°N18'25" 157°W51'30"
Geocentric
Tropical
Placidus
True Node
Rating AA

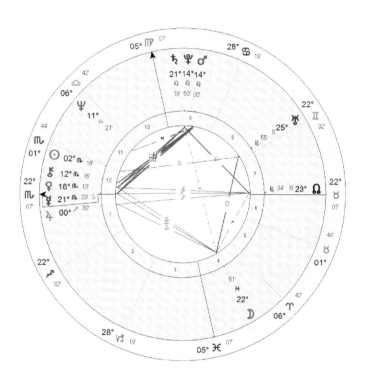

Hilary Clinton
Natal Chart
26 Oct 1947, Sun
8:02 am CST +6:00
chicago, Illinois
41°N51' 087°W39'
Geocentric
Tropical
Placidus
True Node
Rating AA

190

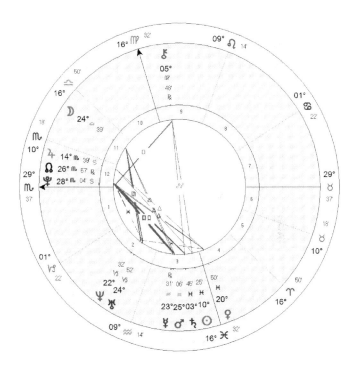

Justin Beiber
Natal Chart
1 Mar 1994 Tue
0:59 am EST +5:00
Stratford, canada
43°N22 080°W57
Geocentric
Tropical
Placidus
True Node
Rating: AA

Taylor Swift – Facebook time
Natal Chart
13 Dec 1989 Wed
8:36 am EST +5:00
Wyomissing Pennsylvania
40°N19'46" 075°W57'56"
Geocentric
Tropical
Placidus
True Node
Rating: AA

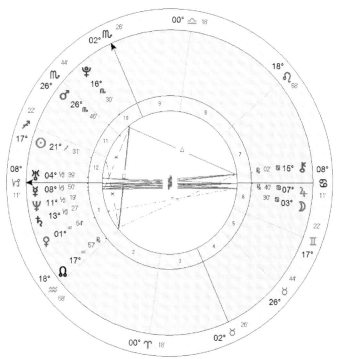

192

Taylor Swift − twittered time
Natal Chart
13 Dec 1989 Wed
8:46 pm EST +5:00
Wyomissing, Pennsylvania
40°N19'46" 075°W57'56"
Geocentric
Tropical
Placidus
True Node
Rating AA

The Horoscope / Natal Chart - the following charts help demonstrate the effects of changes in birth time, date and place on an individual's chart and personality; one hour in time changes the Ascendant by 15⁰ and every other House cusp will change too; the planets move over time, the Moon is the fastest at about 13⁰ per day; the planets move counterclockwise while the outside chart wheel moves clockwise. The Natal Chart of an individual is like a photograph of the planets in the sky with the fixed stars (constellations aka the Signs of the Zodiac) behind them. They appear to be frozen in time. Each planet is placed at a certain degree of a Sign according to where it is in the sky, each Sign rests on a House cusp (unless it falls inside a house). Not all astrological charts are the same.

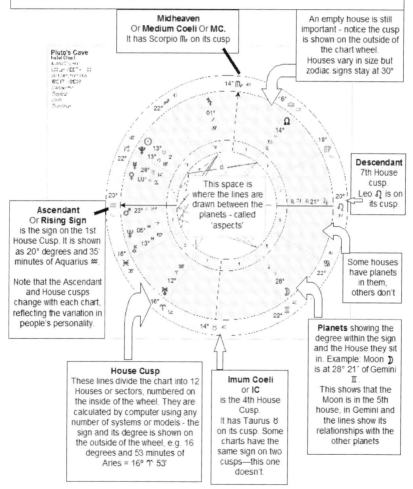

Midheaven
Or **Medium Coeli** Or **MC.**
It has Scorpio ♏ on its cusp

An empty house is still important - notice the cusp is shown on the outside of the chart wheel.
Houses vary in size but zodiac signs stay at 30°

Descendant
7th House cusp.
Leo ♌ is on its cusp.

Ascendant
Or **Rising Sign**
is the sign on the 1st House Cusp. It is shown as 20° degrees and 35' minutes of Aquarius ♒.

Note that the Ascendant and House cusps change with each chart, reflecting the variation in people's personality.

Some houses have planets in them, others don't

This space is where the lines are drawn between the planets - called 'aspects'

House Cusp
These lines divide the chart into 12 Houses or sectors, numbered on the inside of the wheel. They are calculated by computer using any number of systems or models - the sign and its degree is shown on the outside of the wheel, e.g. 16 degrees and 53 minutes of Aries = 16° ♈ 53'

Imum Coeli
or **IC**
is the 4th House Cusp.
It has Taurus ♉ on its cusp. Some charts have the same sign on two cusps—this one doesn't.

Planets showing the degree within the sign and the House they sit in. Example: Moon ☽ is at 28° 21' of Gemini ♊.
This shows that the Moon is in the 5th house, in Gemini and the lines show its relationships with the other planets

Planet	Symbol	Rules	Sign + House	Symbol
Sun	☉	Leo + 5th	Aries / 1	♈
Moon	☽	Cancer + 4th	Taurus / 2	♉
Mercury	☿	Gemini + Virgo 3rd + 6th	Gemini / 3	♊
Venus	♀	Taurus + Libra 2nd + 7th	Cancer / 4	♋
Mars	♂	Aries + 1st	Leo / 5	♌
Jupiter	♃	Sagittarius+9th	Virgo / 6	♍
Saturn	♄	Capricorn+10th	Libra / 7	♎
Chiron	⚷	Nil	Scorpio / 8	♏
Uranus	♅	Aquarius + 11th	Sagittarius/ 9	♐
Neptune	♆	Pisces + 12th	Capricorn/10	♑
Pluto	♇	Scorpio + 8th	Aquarius / 11	♒
North Node	☊	Nil	Pisces / 12	♓

Planet	Symbol	Sign	Symbol
Sun	☉	Aries	♈
Moon	☽	Taurus	♉
Mercury	☿	Gemini	♊
Venus	♀	Cancer	♋
Mars	♂	Leo	♌
Jupiter	♃	Virgo	♍
Saturn	♄	Libra	♎
Chiron	⚷	Scorpio	♏
Uranus	♅	Sagittarius	♐
Neptune	♆	Capricorn	♑
Pluto	♇	Aquarius	♒
North Node	☊	Pisces	♓

About Pluto's Cave Psychological Astrology Series

This book is Part 1 of a series of books on how I combine psychology and astrology. This series consists of :

1. Psychological Astrology and the Twelve Houses
2. Psychological Astrology and the Signs of the Zodiac
3. Psychological Astrology and the Planets of Power

Volumes 2 and 3, coming soon.

Other books by Noel Eastwood:

Astrology of Health: physical and psychological heath in the natal and progressed chart

The Fool's Journey through the Tarot Major Arcana

The Fool's Journey through the Tarot Pentacles

The Fool's Journey through the Tarot Swords

The Fool's Journey through the Tarot Cups

The Fool's Journey through the Tarot Wands

Self Hypnosis Tame Your Inner dragons: clinical and psychic use of trance

If you are interested in learning more about astrology, tarot and how it is intimately linked with psychology please visit my website at www.plutoscave.com

If you liked this book please leave a review, it helps inform readers, and I appreciate your feedback.

Regards,

Noel Eastwood, Psychotherapist, Astrologer, Tarotist

Australia

This edition 2018

About Noel Eastwood & Pluto's Cave

Welcome to Pluto's Cave where be dragons, inner selves and wishing wells.

Noel Eastwood is a retired psychologist who has studied and taught tai chi and taoist meditation, astrology and the tarot for more than 30 years. Pluto's Cave is a metaphor for the hidden world of the unconscious.

Dragons are those invisible yet powerful urges that drive us in predetermined ways. They come from our deep unconscious when we are fearful, angry, sad or uncertain. Dragons can be trained to fly and rejoice in their power, yet few initiates know how to do this.

Inner Selves are parts of our psyche splintered off when bad things happen. These, too, live inside our Cave, our deep Unconscious. They feed our dragons when something triggers unpleasant memories.

Wishing Wells are our treasures, those wondrous potentials that lie hidden deep within. For most, they remain untouched throughout an entire lifetime.

Entering Pluto's Cave is a journey into the unconscious for those who seek to tame their inner Dragons.

In ancient mystery schools, the term 'initiate' is often used to describe the seeker of knowledge. Their quest is to find and rescue, support and nurture their own injured inner self. As many issues arise from childhood traumas, initiates realise that the dragon is in fact their fears. They develop strategies to manage the issues that held them back in life and stunted their relationships. The traumas of the past can indeed be healed.

Initiates delve into 'magic wishing wells' of the mind, places of discovery and wonder. They learn meditation techniques that have been practiced for centuries to control fears and emotions. They dip into these wells to learn more about the meaning of life.

You will learn about these metaphors in his books 'Self Hypnosis Tame Your Inner Dragons' and in his newsletters.

Why not join Noel in your own adventure to heal your soul and uncover your potential?

Subscribe to my weekly newsletter – www.plutoscave.com

Endnotes

[1] *As You Like It* Act 2, scene 7, 139–143.

[2] not her real name

[3] an Australian monitor lizard

[4] Joseph Campbell

Made in the USA
San Bernardino, CA
14 December 2018